I hope you enjoy!

Our Frugal Summer in Charente

An Expat's Kitchen Garden Journal

By

Sarah Jane Butfield

Copyright ©2014 Sarah Jane Butfield

Cover design Nigel Butfield

Photography by Nigel Butfield

First ebook and paperback editions October 2014

Second ebook & paperback editions October 2016

ISBN: 978-1503080362

The people and events in this book are portrayed as perceived and experienced by Sarah Jane Butfield. The moral right of the author has been asserted. All rights reserved.

No part of this book may be reproduced, stored in a retrieval system or transmitted without written permission of the publisher.

Dedication

Acknowledgments

Introduction

Index of recipes

Preface - What is this book about?

Chapter 1 February

Chapter 2 March

Chapter 3 April

Chapter 4 May

Chapter 5 June

Chapter 6 July

Chapter 7 August

Chapter 8 September

Chapter 9 October

Chapter 10 Preparing for Christmas

About the Author:

Books by Sarah Jane Butfield

Dedication

This book is dedicated to my late Mother

Muriel Maud McDonald.

(1936 – 1992)

Always in my thoughts.

Acknowledgements

Firstly, I would like to thank my extremely tolerant husband Nigel, not only for his contributions to this book, but also for his hard work in our secret garden in Charente.

Thank you to my family for their continued support of both my writing projects and my new publishing venture. Social media participation is a key component to building an author platform. Therefore every tweet and status share means a great deal to authors. Family and friends who have shared and interacted with myself and the members of the Rukia Publishing Team during book promotion events are very much appreciated, so thank you.

Finally I would also like to thank beta reader and proofreader Martin Papworth for his valued feedback and input to this book which has enhanced its production.

Introduction

Welcome to Our Frugal Summer in Charente: An Expat's Kitchen Garden Journal.

I have a passion for living simply, and I believe that it can lead to a more sustainable and healthier lifestyle. In this book I wanted to capture the process that Nigel and I went through, as well as describing the results we achieved. In reality it was not a lifestyle decision to live a more frugal existence, it was a necessity. However, we enjoyed the challenge. On a tight budget we did not always have the correct ingredients, so a degree of improvisation, which is my specialty in the kitchen, came into force. I am not well known for my cooking abilities, although I am renowned for my culinary catastrophes. Many of my friends and family find it amusing that I not only managed to cook in a house with no kitchen but that I made and adapted recipes without poisoning either myself or Nigel in the process. Although I admit we came close with the wild mushrooms, but more on that story later!

Welcome to the Charente.

Sarah Jane

Index of Recipes

MINT SAUCE

MEDITERRANEAN OLIVE COBBLE BREAD

NETTLE TEA

NETTLE SOUP

RHUBARB JAM

CHEESE AND LEEK JACKET POTATOES

JAIME'S VERSION OF TEENAGE WEDGES

MCJAIME HASH BROWNS

PICKLING BEETROOT

GARLIC AND HERB SAUTÉED COURGETTE FLOWERS

ELDERFLOWER CORDIAL

CHICKEN ONE POT MEAL

BUDGET LEFTOVERS MEAL

PLUM JAM

BLACKBERRY JAM

CHIRAC CIDER

COURGETTE WINE

FIG BISCUITS

Sarah Jane Butfield

COURGETTE CAKE

CURRIED COURGETTE CHUTNEY

SHEILA'S MARROW RUM

SPINACH AND LEEK OMELETTE

BACON AND SPINACH FRITTATA

LUXURY FISH PIE WITH ROSTI TOPPING

BUBBLE AND SQUEAK

COURGETTE AND POTATO SOUP

VEGETABLE CURRY

SWEETCORN PATTIES

PUMPKIN CURRY

PUMPKIN DUMPLINGS

CHESTNUT LOAF

CHESTNUT AND RED WINE PATE

SARAH JANE'S BREAD SAUCE

Our Frugal Summer in Charente
An Expat's Kitchen Garden Journal.
Preface - What is this book about?

This book details our journey through the summer of 2013 in the Charente, South West France. After relocating from Australia to France in September 2012, we soon found ourselves enduring desperate times. We realised that the only way we could continue our new life in France was if we lived in a frugal, more conservative manner. Our plan was to save money by any means possible, to enable us to invest any money we could earn into renovating the house. There were prolonged periods when Nigel was unable to find regular work and we were living in a house that needed upgrading into some degree of habitability. Our savings or renovation fund was evaporating fast into the proverbial money pit, which is an expat term for a renovation project. On a practical level my contribution to our situation was by utilising every inch of our garden, in true 'Good Life' style. I would achieve this by keeping some chickens, ducks and growing enough vegetables to feed ourselves and the animals. The learning curve to ensure that we made the most of everything we produced in our garden was huge. We also utilised foraged foods from the hedgerows for making teas, jams and nutty delights. I can say with all honesty, without meaning to sound as if I am bragging that we have had some delicious food and drink as a result of our efforts and resourcefulness.

The idea for this book came from reviewing some of the recipes in my journal that I adapted over this thrifty period living in our new French home. We were surviving on a minimal budget, trying to feed ourselves from our vegetable garden, five chickens and two ducks. A cookbook written in wartime inspired some of my frugal adaptations of family friendly recipes. The 'Come into the garden cookbook' by Constance Spry gives the feeling of extravagant recipes while adhering to and speaking of, wartime rations and availability. Some of the content for this book comes from my journals, just like my two travel memoirs Glass Half Full: Our Australian Adventure and Two dogs and suitcase: Clueless in Charente.

Therefore, it is probably no surprise that this has turned into the story of my kitchen garden and other animals rather than a recipe book. The feedback received while preparing this book made me realise that some of the recipes I added had funny anecdotes and stories behind them and so I have shared some of those with you too.

**Our 'potager' week one –
Grass cut ready to start our Good Life project**

The French tradition of using produce from their 'potager', or kitchen garden, is renowned for enabling French families to create meals that are healthy, cost effective and simple. They select the plants they grow with skill and precision based on years of knowledge passed down through the generations. The result is a variety of fruits and vegetables that can provide year round nutritious meals for their families. In my last book I shared with you recipes for; wild boar marinade, green tomato chutney, Chirac cheesy scones, pizza dough, radish relish and courgette cake. The interest in the recipes and our garden activities led me to change the layout of this book. Therefore, I decided to arrange this book in a month by month format to incorporate some of the practicalities of our kitchen garden setup. As promised in my last book I have included the recipes for chestnut loaf, pumpkin curry, pumpkin pie and pumpkin dumplings together with luxury fish pie and fig biscuits. I have also added others that I hope you will enjoy. I have no formal catering expertise, other than that learned in my school and adult life, and this is purely my guide.

This book details how we grew, foraged and cooked with home-grown fresh fruits and vegetables over the spring and summer of 2013. It describes how in our small 'potager' we produced enough food to survive in France, while still eating a healthy nutritious diet.

I learned new skills in bread making, cooking and preserving, which in turn reduced our expenditure in the supermarket. It also had an environmental impact as we produced less packaging waste for the fortnightly recycle truck. I think at one point they thought we had moved away! The art of enjoying the simple things in life like family, friends, and a home-grown and home-cooked meal is very rewarding.

Therefore, I hope that if you bought this book for the recipes, that you enjoy making them. If you are curious about how an English woman in France made a very small food budget go a long way, then I hope you find it informative and at times amusing. If you just like reading about anything and, everything to do with France then enjoy the ride. As a longstanding fan of the 1970's television show 'The Good Life' we have often tried to create our version of the good life in small ways in various locations. However, it was not until we moved to live in rural outback Queensland, Australia that I had my first large scale attempt. Here in France this is my second full blown attempt at a more organic, self-sufficient lifestyle. We have eaten organic produce, whenever possible, since our vegetarian and vegan days in Australia. Once you experience organically produced crops the differentiation in flavour is hard to ignore, especially when you return to eating mass produced vegetables in particular. Therefore to be able to grow our own near organic produce was an exciting challenge.

Nigel and I attempted a degree of self-sufficiency armed with a vegetable patch reclaimed from a garden that resembled a meadow and measured just 50 feet in length. There was also an area of the garden, unsuitable for vegetables because the ground housed the roots of the trees that lined the brook that runs along the perimeter. Another patch had the remains of an outhouse that had long since crumbled to the ground. This area we converted into a duck and chicken enclosure. We started with a small chest freezer and about sixty jars collected from friends and neighbours.

Our aim was to ensure that our freezer would be full of produce for winter. We also wanted there to be plenty of jams, pickles, preserves together with cold store vegetables such as onions, garlic, potatoes and pumpkins in the barn. 'Enough to feed a small army' as Nigel would say.

The word 'frugal' became our buzzword over this period of our lives. We applied it not only to the purchase or production of the ingredients, but also to the use of them to maintain a healthy diet. We set out to ensure that we made the most of everything we bought, grew or raised. The art of learning to use every edible part of our garden produce has been a delicious experiment as well as an education. The discovery that we could make a drastic reduction in our food bill without compromising on variety, taste or nutrition was like learning a new language. A language that you always admired, but never had the confidence to try. As a novice cook that was my take on how I would approach the task in hand.

I hope to share some of the lessons we learned, the mistakes we made and some of the tips that we picked up from experimenting and sharing the knowledge acquired from my new friends and neighbours. As I look back on the food, both produced and cooked, that we enjoyed over the summer of 2013 I believe that the success of achieving a frugal or thrifty use of food comes down to mindfulness. We live in a throwaway society relying, for the most part, on convenience in some form. Waste is increasing because of over buying, poor storage, short shelf life and lack of education. In relation to food, it doesn't need to be that way. In my teenage years in our home economics class we learned not only about food and cooking methods but how to buy while checking for ripeness and quality, how to store and preserve. We are more capable of utilizing food to its maximum than we sometimes believe or acknowledge. However, time plays a big part in that and as, we can all perceive ourselves as time poor at certain times, organisation is the key to success in reducing your food bill while enjoying some tasty food. The ability to use food in its totality, recycling leftovers and being creative enables you to make the most of your food budget. It doesn't have to be a chore; it is a craft. As with any craft it takes time and practice to perfect it, but once learned you can apply it to many areas and create wonderful things.

As with most things in life today we feel the need to label things. The downside of labelling is that whatever label you apply someone will object or question it. To avoid that, I suggest that we do not call this a cookbook. By definition, a cookbook is "a kitchen reference publication that typically contains a collection of recipes" and as I am not a cook that doesn't seem an appropriate label or reference point. I prefer to call it an expat journey into gardening and cooking on a budget in rural South West France. It is our story of experimenting, learning and enjoying one long hot summer in our French cottage garden.

Enter the garden, explore, enjoy and eat well.

Chapter 1
February

The foundations of our new lifestyle, dug quite literally.

The work begins to create a garden suitable to grow vegetables and to keep some small livestock, namely chickens. Since October 2012 we have cleared the rubble, brambles, bushes and small trees which have taken over the garden during its years of vacancy. My romantic imagery comes to the fore again as I name this my secret garden. My secret garden, littered with the scars of neglect, will be brought back to life. That is where the romantic imagery finishes; because it will not be the host of flowers and shrubs instead it will accommodate vegetables, fruit bushes and a variety of animals. I have drafted out a plan of action for planting, well a crude pencil drawing which is not to scale and as such Nigel is not impressed with it.

"Unrealistic" is how he described my action plan saying, "Is that really how a woman perceives feet and inches!"

Nigel accepts the challenge of completing the first dig which will be no easy task as this garden has clearly not been dug for many years. We do not have a mechanical digging machine or rotavator, like our French neighbours. André even has a tractor and plough, which is a bit over the top, although he is 85 years old, so I think he has earned some help with the way he prepares his soil.

We have just a garden spade and a fork, but undeterred we are going to dig all the way from outside the barn to approximately 2 feet away from the brook the end of the garden. In total, this is about 50 feet! The garden is now forming into two sections. The area behind the barn is becoming the vegetable garden and the area behind the house will house the animal enclosures. I know it will appear strange and irresponsible, although we have no choice in reality, but we need to house the boys, our dogs, Dave and Buster, in the enclosure closest to the house. However, this will mean they are adjacent to the chickens. I am sure we have fun times ahead dealing with that.

Our boys; Dave on the left and Buster on the right.

Dave and Buster are Australian cattle dogs. They joined the Butfield family in Alice Springs; Dave in 2008 and Buster in 2009. In a twist of fate we found Buster at an RSPCA centre in Alice Springs and later found out that he came from the same litter as Dave.

In our garden, month by month, new seeds will be sown. New areas will be cultivated, and as spring becomes summer, the crops will be harvested in earnest. Well, that's the plan. As an amateur gardener, I was attempting to grow plants from seeds bought in France. Seeds that came in packets and which required the translation of the instructions using my trusted French to English dictionary. For anyone who has ever tried this, many of the words on the packets don't appear in the dictionary.

As we didn't have access to the internet at this time I didn't have the option of using Google translate to help me, so in all honesty mistakes were made.

Sarah Jane's Secret Garden Action Plan

Here is the month by month planting and harvesting schedule, although other vegetables did end up being planted when we were given plants or seeds by friends and neighbours:

February - Plant onion sets and garlic (tomatoes were started indoors.)

March - Plant early new potatoes, courgettes, egg-plants (aubergines), cabbage, cauliflower, beetroot, lettuce, spinach, peas, leeks and pumpkins.

April - Plant sweetcorn, more pumpkins, leeks, lettuce and radishes.

May - Plant broccoli, strawberries, lettuce, radish and peas.

June - Plant haricot verte (dried beans from André from his successful year.)

July - Plant the second batch of new potatoes.

August - Harvest haricot verte, peas and strawberries.

September - Harvest leeks and courgettes.

October - Harvest pumpkins and the remaining courgettes.

Now straightaway I can visualise all the more experienced gardeners reading this and grimacing at the early or late planting and the combination of crops. However, in my defence as I said at the outset I am not a chef or a gardener. I am just a crazy expat English woman who wants to achieve her version of 'The Good Life'. This was my attempt, and I am not advocating that it is in any way the correct or only way to achieve results, but it is the method I used with some success.

While Nigel commenced digging, I started the huge task of weeding. The grass, stinging nettles and dandelion roots take their toll on my hands, but it is all for the greater good as we keep saying whenever we suffer an injury or discomfort of some description. As we do not have a greenhouse, and the downstairs of the house is as yet inhabitable, I am creating a hothouse in Jaime's bedroom at the back of the house. It gets hot in the morning as the sun radiates through the extremely thin old glass of our French windows. It generates a great deal of heat even in this very cold month of February. I have some seed trays which we found in the barn during the first stage of clearing, and I have planted spinach and herbs so far.

Whenever we move, be it international or interstate, we always seem to restart with herbs when we arrive, whether it is planting them or buying them for the store cupboard.

I suppose it's because we were vegetarian for such a long time, and herbs for flavouring were key to ensuring that whatever vegetable dish we made it is one that you will remember favourably. Just as you have mint sauce with lamb or sage and onion with chicken, there are certain herbs that enhance the taste of vegetables. Herbs that we have found and used in vegetarian dishes that go well together, in the same way from our experimentation include:

Potatoes with garlic, basil, mint or sage

Cabbage with mint

Carrots with sage

Sweet Corn with thyme, basil and rosemary

Broccoli with basil and chives

Peas with thyme

Green beans with basil, chestnuts and garlic

Eggplant (aubergine) with parsley

Brussel Sprouts with chestnuts

Spinach with garlic and lemon juice

The art of combining and cooking herbs and vegetables can result in achieving unforgettable meals and dishes. The trick I think is not to go for extreme or fancy herbs and spices, but to stick to the common ones which are easy to source and grow. A supply of herbs, such as oregano, basil, parsley, thyme, rosemary, coriander and dill, can transform even the blandest looking vegetable platter. If you then add ingredients like ginger, garlic, lemon-grass, cinnamon and nutmeg, there is no end to the flavours you can create. As well as flavour, herbs can add texture to vegetable dishes, in the same way as adding grated or chopped nuts.

On our frugal budget, wanting to maximise the production from our vegetable garden, you will notice that I only grew a small range of herbs. These included basil, parsley, coriander, chives, sage, thyme, mint. I would encourage you to experiment with whatever you have growing or stored in the cupboard. Dried herbs work just as well although you need less I find as they can have a stronger flavour. The use of herbs can turn your meals into an appetising food experience in addition to supporting good health as they are also rich in vitamins and nutrients.

As we made our way through the garden bringing to life freshly dug rich soil ready for planting, we collected twigs and sticks for building pea and bean support frameworks and tomato plant support sticks. It was then that we came across some prolific mint. The iconic odour had embraced our senses before we had even seen it in its full splendour. This valuable resource could not be wasted. We made homemade mint sauce the same night.

Mint sauce

Ingredients:

50g sugar

150g malt vinegar

Large bunch of fresh mint leaves

Method:

Chop the mint before adding it to the blender.

Blend the sugar and vinegar with the mint for 2-3 minutes.

Pour the mixture into a bowl and set aside for 15 minutes until the sugar is fully dissolved.

We put ours into sterilised jam jars for storage and a small portion, left over which did not fill a complete jar, was placed in the fridge for use over the next four weeks.

With care, although obviously as it was growing untendered before we arrived we didn't need to be too careful, we pruned the mint back and contained it with garden string so that we could plant other herbs around it. As we continued the clearing, as if magically positioned there, we came across some wild chives. 'Gifts from the Gods,' I called them, as Nigel rolled his eyes as he does when I say things like that. Some of the chives had gone to seed, but we sampled the remainder. It was very strong, and we knew instantly it would make an excellent accompaniment to many meals that are normally enhanced by either onion or garlic. The act of harvesting fresh chives in February was quite surreal, and we didn't want to waste any of them, so we froze them, in ice cube trays with olive oil poured over them. When we needed them, we could just pop out a cube or two and use them to sauté vegetables or to add to a mince dish like spaghetti bolognaise.

Snow covered vegetable garden

On 8th February the snow arrived and this cut short my gardening activity, therefore I turned to completing another French homely bucket list item, that of attempting to bake bread. Ok, I had to buy the flour and yeast, but I was making bread from scratch. No bread-machine or food-processor, just painstaking kneading of the dough, plenty of hoping and a little prayer.

French bread.

I dabbled in bread making several times over the years despite an inauspicious debut during my Home Economic O'Level practical examination in 1980. My practical examination consisted of planning, preparing and serving a three-course meal. The starter I planned was vegetable soup with the vegetables coming from my grandmother's garden. I felt confident that the quality alone would add to the success of this dish. The accompaniment to this delicious homemade soup would be freshly baked bread rolls. With my bread roll recipe researched and ready for action in blissful teenage ignorance as the recipe said it was 'simple' I saw no need to practice it beforehand.

On the day, I planned everything to time with military precision, knowing that I needed to make the bread first as it need time to rise. With the bread dough prepared and put to one side under a warm damp tea towel, I continued with the other dishes. When the time came to bake the bread rolls, I was disappointed to see that they hadn't risen as indicated in the recipe instructions. Undeterred I glazed the tops with the beaten egg and baked them for the required time. When they were cooked, although small, they looked the part. Golden brown shiny top and perfectly round. I served them in a basket lined with a napkin beside my soup in a rustic brown tureen and felt quite pleased with myself.

When the examiner reached my table, she went to cut into one of the rolls and imagine my embarrassment as it shot across the table breaking my display wine glasses in the process. Not to be beaten by a knife the examiner picked another roll and attempted to break it open with her hands, tear 'n share style. When this too was unsuccessful, she decided to progress on to the main course. At the end of the examination, I packaged up my soup into a flask and my bread rolls into a plastic container. I added them to my other meal components in the straw basket my mum had lent me. When I got home my sisters were eager to sample my creations, however the soup had solidified into a thick sludge which obstinately refused to exit the flask. The bread rolls which no one could bite into were tossed around like cricket balls and even our dog Rex, an Alsatian cross, could not penetrate them. It is now a long-standing family joke that when I mention bread making, and especially when I mention writing this book that they remind me of this story and its credentials in relation to my culinary skills.

This experience has not affected my enthusiasm for bread making. While living in Australia, both in the woods in Queensland and in cosmopolitan Hobart, Tasmania I resurrected my craft. In Hobart my good friend Anna, who is of Italian origin, introduced me to a French patisserie called Daci & Daci. They always hosted an extensive array of cakes, breads and pastries which required no persuasion to sample. Inspired by their olive cobble loaf, I attempted my version with great success. I brought this successful recipe with me to France in the sure knowledge that I would recreate this Mediterranean delicacy to eat in my rustic kitchen garden with some cheese and fine wine.

Mediterranean olive cobble loaf perfect with cheese

Ingredients:

500g bread flour

1 tsp salt

2 tbsp olive oil

1 tsp sugar

7g sachet of easy yeast or 15 g of fresh yeast

300ml warm water

150g black Greek olives, pitted and chopped.

Method:

Put the flour into a mixing bowl and add the salt and sugar.

For fresh yeast, crumble it and rub into the flour like adding margarine when making pastry.

With easy-blend dried yeast simply stir this into the flour, salt and sugar mixture.

Measure 100 ml of boiling water into a measuring jug adding a further 200 ml of cold water. Make sure it is warm, and not hot, by testing the temperature with your finger then add the olive oil.

Make a well in the dry ingredients in the bowl and add the liquid a little at a time.

Working the ingredients in with a fork, it will quickly form a sticky dough. Make sure you wipe the dough around the bowl to catch all the ingredients.

Work the ingredients together with your hands and transfer it to a floured surface and start kneading the dough until it is shiny and pliable.

Put the prepared dough back into the mixing bowl and cover with a damp tea towel and leave to rest for 1 hr.

Pull the dough into two and in each piece add half of the olives before re-joining the two pieces and forming a round shape like a big bun. Sprinkle with flour lightly on the top and with a sharp knife mark a cross.

Place the dough ball on a baking tray lined with baking paper and leave it for one hour in a warm place. Bake at 220C/425F/Gas 7 for 30 minutes until golden brown. Remove from the oven and place on a cooling rack.

Fortunately in France olives were cheap, and they liven up any bread mixture and give you the impression of extravagance while eating and cooking on a budget. The challenges encountered with bread making in France came firstly in the form of finding the right yeast. Even though I carried my trusty English to French dictionary in the baking aisle, I still managed to mix up the yeasts, resulting in me ending up with brioche which resulted in sweet tasting bread, instead of normal bread.

Secondly, trying to perfect the right temperature to get the bread to rise, i.e. windowsill, under or near the wood burner or in the garden was a challenge depending on the time of year.

First bread left to prove under woodburner

When the log burner was alight the heat from it produced the best results. However, one day in the summer I placed the dough on the tin roof of the dog enclosure and forgot to get it in before we went into Chabanais. When we came home, it was like a scene from the 1958 and 1988 horror movie 'The Blob'. The mutant like dough had escaped the bowl and was making its way across the hot tin roof like lava escaping from a volcano.

The third challenge was finding suitable bread flour. Obviously on a budget we opted for the blue label own brand basic flour. 90% of the time, this, with a little extra salt and extra kneading time, was perfectly adequate. However, when I tried to cut corners on busy days to save time the result was flat dry bread which only the chickens would eat.

As homemade bread, with no preservatives, goes stale quicker than shop-bought bread I made the end of loaves into breadcrumbs and froze them ready for use in homemade bread sauce for Christmas. The homemade bread was sometimes difficult to slice efficiently, so it became important to find alternatives to sandwiches. In turn, this led me to, over the summer, to create a variety of vegetable-based soups, which are perfect for the dipping of homemade bread. There will be more on seasonal soups in later chapters.

Perfecting the bread -making

On the 15th and 28th February after the recent snow had finally cleared the cranes flew over. On both occasions, it was a sunny afternoon with clear blue skies. We had heard them before we saw their iconic V shape formation appear from over the barn as they headed towards Chabanais. We had heard that this is the first sign that spring has sprung. With spring on the way my gardening calendar looks like this:

The beginnings of a vegetable garden

Planted outdoors: - 3 rows of onions, 4 rows of garlic. Planted indoors: - plum tomato seeds and herbs (basil, coriander and Italian parsley.)

With my seeds ready and a plan of action made for March, it's full steam ahead for a busy expat kitchen gardener.

Chapter 2
March

March arrived with a flurry of activity in the garden, and our early planted onions and garlic were already breaking the ground, much to the dismay of our French neighbours who still fear the frosts. In the garden, we added to their garden horrors by pruning back, quite harshly by some people's standards. But then people who do not know Nigel will not know what he is like when he handles a pair of loppers he is renowned for getting carried away. This fact can be confirmed by our friends Tim and Nicky after they let him loose on a hedge once!

Bay tree pruning commences

Behind the bread oven when we arrived there was a huge, but dead looking bay tree. We love bay leaves, and Nigel insists on using them when he cooks his signature dish, spaghetti bolognaise. He should have been the cook here in France as he at least has some professional experience to draw on, whereas I make it up as I go along. We had already, last October, taken off a lot of the top and side branches of the bay tree, but decided to leave it at that as winter was approaching. It was not until our initial cull had commenced that we noticed that all of the houses on our side of the street had a bay tree in the garden. They all looked dead, but no one else was pruning. Were we making a mistake here? Undeterred we continued. However, now we are into spring, and the supposedly dead trees have taken off again and ours was causing cracks in the bread oven wall. The ivy that had crept up the narrow bay tree truck had infiltrated the stone wall behind the tree removing its soft sand mortar. As we carefully removed the ivy, we realised it was not enough and that we needed to cut the bay tree back further.

We did not want to waste any of the bay leaves so the branches were cut off and put near the back door so that we could pick every leaf off ready to store for future use. The branches would be stored in the barn to season as next year's firewood. How do you even store bay leaves? Fortunately, the issue of how to store bay leaves is a popular subject and was featured in one of the questions and answer pages of the gardening magazines. Therefore, the plan was to 'pick the leaves off and lay them to dry in a warm, airy room'. As I read this my eyes rolled as thoughts of 'where in this building site of a home can I find somewhere to do that, we have thousands of leaves here'. Even if I gave bundles of bay leaves away there were too many unless I could devise a drying system. We decided to keep some fresh in clip top plastic boxes for immediate use, and they kept fresh for three months.

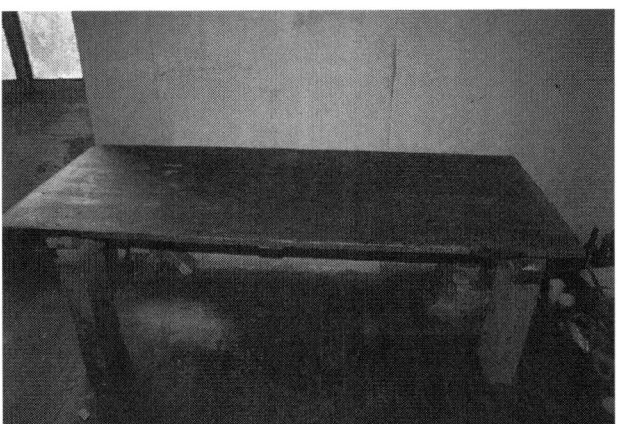

Homemade table

In the meantime, Jaime and I decided to construct a makeshift drying table from an old wooden door placed on piles of bricks in her bedroom. Voila! All we needed to do then was layer it with newspapers and leaves. It was like doing a big green jigsaw puzzle, but with no picture. The aim was to cover the newspaper. When the leaves were dry, approximately two weeks later, we placed them into air-tight plastic food containers for storage and later use. Problem solved we would have bay leaves for every meal!

I started planting out my courgettes, egg-plants (aubergines,) cabbage and cauliflower seedlings which I started off in Jaime's bedroom. The cucumbers, also propagated indoors, and some of my herbs are upgraded to larger pots as they are still too fragile to be planted out. However, some of the more hardy herbs like my Italian parsley and rosemary are big enough to be transplanted into the stony area set aside for herbs near to the back door. This would enable easy access from the kitchen or our al-fresco bread oven when we were cooking.

Also in March we acquired our five, two-week-old chickens, after being assured by the French lady at the vide grenier where we bought them that they would be laying eggs by July. For now, they had to live indoors as they were very small, and the chicken wire enclosure that Nigel had started would not stop them from escaping or protect them from being attacked by foxes.

Four of the five chicks, named after the Spice Girls

The chickens take up residence in Jaime's bedroom alongside her rabbit Rosie. I know how this sounds but our house was a building site, and it was the safest place for them. Various defences were erected in the doorways and around trailing wires, etc. Nigel and Jaime made temporary perches for them to sit on both in a large cardboard box enclosure and in the corner of the room for when they were free roaming. It was a bit messy at times and copious amounts of newspapers from friends and neighbours were employed to prevent soiling of our oak floorboards. Even so we knew that the boards would need to be sanded before varnishing when the renovation work was complete. My worry was the smell whereas Jaime was more concerned about her One Direction posters which the chickens liked to peck at!

Towards the end of March, the weather was glorious and as over two weeks had passed with no frost, I was feeling brave enough to expand my planting plan. As Nigel's double digging of the vegetable patch neared completion, I began planting; cabbages, beetroot, lettuce, spinach, peas, leeks and pumpkins. Double digging is a gardening term I had often heard, but never really understood the need for or relevance of. We had started reading old copies of BBC Gardeners World magazines which we acquired from beside a recycling bin in Confolens. I didn't consider that act to be stealing because they were left to be recycled, and I was recycling them by reading them! Apparently double digging was needed when the soil had been uncultivated for some time, and the drainage needed to be improved. However, as Nigel will attest to, it was a time-consuming and back-breaking process. But as I kept telling him 'it's all for the greater good' and all of his back breaking hard work would be rewarded with an abundance of crops.

I hoped I would be able to deliver on that promise as he looked unimpressed at the time as he surveyed my barren looking plot. I decided to make it look more productive and garden-like by erecting sticks with little flags at the ends of each line of seeds planted. I noticed during this process that I was already running out of garden space in which to plant according to my plan. Had I spaced the crops properly? I hoped so, because Nigel said the plants and rows were too close together. However, I couldn't risk wasted space, and my plan B was that if I saw gaps as the crops came up I would fill them with seedlings from indoors.

The developing vegetable garden

With the help of André's over 60 years' experience in growing vegetables, I was quickly educated to many gardening facts, the most important of which was that as we harvested our crops we had to rotate the below and above the ground plants for ultimate soil efficiency. As we continued with the outdoor planting, it was already obvious that our seeds and seedlings were not alone in the garden when we retreated to our little cottage overnight. There was early morning evidence of slugs having left their silvery trails glistening in the morning sun on the wooden temporary decking, which Nigel had placed outside the back door to stop me tripping over the rubble. Upon closer inspection, they were consuming the spinach as fast as it was emerging from the ground. As we did not want to use chemicals we tried the old fashioned methods of crushed egg shells, salt and beer buried in yoghurt pots, all of which were successful to a degree but we were out-numbered.

We would not admit defeat or give in, so I started more seeds in trays indoors and planted out the replacements to counteract this slug feeding frenzy. Would I ever get ahead of them? The answer was a resounding yes as we started the second phase of our organic pest control. After manual picking of the slugs each morning and evening the plants were sprayed with our grey waste water. We used an eco-washing up liquid which ironically is cheaper than the conventional ones here in France which is unusual. As we had no bathroom our nightly strip wash with our trusty pink buckets produced plenty of water to fill the spray bottles. By the end of March, the slugs were either dead or had retreated. Again such was my naivety, what had actually happened was that the hedgehogs had arrived, much to Dave and Buster's annoyance at night time.

Therefore, the layout of the garden, thus far working from the house toward the brook at the perimeter of the garden plan looked like this:

Grape vine and tomato plants

Tomatoes and grapes against the wall of the barn; three rows each of spinach, leeks and lettuce; three rows of potatoes; two rows of peas; a one metre square cabbage patch. Where the garden meets the pre-existing blackcurrant bush, which I had pruned hopeful of reviving it for summer, I had made one meter square areas for each of the following: beetroot, cauliflower and sweetcorn. The green beans, or haricot verte as they are called in France, which need supporting, will grow along the side of the footpath. The framework made of sticks and string formed a pattern that resembled the children's game 'cat's cradle'.

The courgettes and pumpkins which could cope in rougher ground were planted near the brook in the rooty earth still littered with pottery and stones from the clearing of the outhouse. The other crop already in residence and growing profusely was the stinging nettles.

Nettle patch by the babbling brook

As I contemplated scything them and then digging out the root system I was reminded by Nigel that nettle tea was good for my hay fever. When we lived in Cornwall, we had also made and eaten nettle soup. It was a free food source, and when times were hard, we could not waste this precious commodity. Here are the recipes for both the nettle tea and soup.

Nettle tea is renowned for help with asthma and alleviating most respiratory issues. Wherever you pick, your nettles always wash them thoroughly before using them. They have hairy leaves which trap dirt, dust and other undesirable additional ingredients if you are not careful!

Nettle Tea

Ingredients

Nettles - the tips are best for making the tea as the large leaves do not produce a strong enough flavour, so just snip the tips off with scissors.

Method

Roughly chop them and place in a saucepan or cafetière.

For the saucepan method - add one cup of water to one cup of nettles in the saucepan and bring the water to the boil.

Cafetière - for 2 cups of tea add 2 cups of nettles to the cafetière, then add 2 cups of boiling water and allow it too steep for 10 minutes.

Nettle soup

When collecting nettles for use in soup, I had read that it was best to use nettles before they flower, which in UK was around May, so I anticipated it would be slightly earlier here in France. Obviously you need to wear gloves and remember to protect your ankles and upper arms because if they are exposed to the nettles the irritation can be immense.

Ingredients:

500g nettles- torn or cut in shreds

1 tsp olive oil

1 onion chopped finely

1 carrot chopped

1 potato cubed

1 pint vegetable stock

500g nettles

2 tbsp of cream or milk

Method:

In a large saucepan, add the oil and put it on low heat. Spoon in the chopped onion, carrot, and potato, and cook for about 15 minutes until the potato cubes start to soften.

Pour in the vegetable stock and simmer for a further 10 minutes until the potato is cooked.

Add the nettle leaves, and simmer until the nettles have wilted like spinach. Season to taste, and then blend for 2 minutes, before stirring in the cream or milk.

Nigel liked to garnish his soup with more dead nettles, but I do not like the idea of putting them in my mouth uncooked, and I had visions of it resulting in a swollen irritated tongue. Therefore, I preferred to drizzle some extra olive oil on mine and garnish with Italian parsley. As horrible as nettle soup may sound and look, after all we were eating weeds, it was delicious. It kept us in lunchtime soups until something grew in the garden that I could make a proper meal with!

Chapter 3
April

On the 1st April 2013 the sunshine had returned, and my planting resumed.

Vegetable growth starts, thank goodness!

The onions and garlic were established and the courgettes had already sprouted and by the 4th the cabbage plants were poking their green shoots through as well. It was reassuring to see something happening. Even though I knew it would happen, there was always the fear that all the hard work and effort had been in vain. I loved springtime and being back in Europe to enjoy it. Springtime always brings back happy memories from my childhood. I started to notice the cowslips in the ditches, and daffodils and crocuses on the grass verge as we drove towards Confolens and Chabanais to collect building supplies or do the food shopping. Buds appeared on the trees around our garden and on the roadside. Local farmers were preparing their fields and fences, and a general sense of activity prevailed. As I started to see and recognise plants, flowers, trees and springtime activities, some of which were not present in Australia, until now I had not realised how much I had missed them.

In the mornings, the spring sunshine dazzled me as it reflected on my newly cleaned glass panel windows. I was very pleased with the results of using white vinegar and newspaper, an old fashioned trick that my mum taught me in my youth. However, the neighbours looked on as I cleaned the windows with some suspicion.

'That crazy expat woman, why is she rubbing the windows with newspapers?' The sunshine also reflected from the French roof tiles of the buildings opposite the house. The roof tiles, which appeared irregular in colour and shape, were a variety of shades of browns and reds. This was highlighted as it was in stark contrast to the clear blue sky which had remained cloudless for the whole of the first week of April.

Roving seed trays.

In the glorious sunshine, I returned to my gardening projects. My seedling pots and trays were seriously in the way in Jaime's bedroom, despite being moved outside whenever possible to harden them, now that the chickens and the rabbit needed room to move as well. I developed a process of moving the trays hourly to try to capture the morning sun. One morning Nigel decided that we had outgrown this morning manoeuvring activity and that some form of greenhouse or cloche in the garden was needed. He discussed the idea with Tim, whom he was working with for three days a week, and the following day he came home with six old French windows from a house where they were working.

They were all long and thin in shape with brightly coloured, yet flaking paint, in blues, reds and greens. I did not need any encouragement to transfer my seedlings into the cloche as soon as it was assembled, which I made Nigel do after work that evening. Even Jaime helped to move the plants because it meant one less obstacle in her bedroom. In the cloche now were the next set of lettuces, tomato plants, cucumbers and cabbages.

The garden was filling nicely according to my plan, and work had started on the chicken enclosure. The chicks were still in Jaime's bedroom and were growing fast and becoming more annoying both to us and the rabbit. If Nigel's work on the enclosure continued to go to plan we expected to be able to transfer them to the garden in May.

The birds in the garden are in full and glorious song from early in the morning now that spring is in full swing. One particular day, after I had spent the whole day pottering around in the garden, Nigel came home from work, and we sat in our evening sitting position near the barn on our plastic chairs. A bird started singing.

"Did you hear that?"

"What?" Nigel said, with a slight frown indicating his annoyance at my verbal interruption of his quiet relaxation time.

"That bird singing. Do you recognise the tune?"

Nigel looked down his nose at me like a school teacher about to correct his pupil. All he needed was a pair of glasses perched on his nose, and the image would have been perfect. "Birds don't sing a tune they can't read music."

"I know that silly, but don't you think it sounds like the song Richard Briers used to whistle in the good life? I have been listening to it all day, but I just can't think of the name of it."

"I don't think that the tune he whistled even had a name, haven't we talked or looked into this before?"

I returned to my thoughts and recollections on this matter, still listening to the birds singing.

"I think you wonder too much," says Nigel now breaking into my silent thinking time. "Maybe you need an IPod; you are obviously spending far too much time having conversations with yourself, the boys and the chicks about fictional tunes during the day."

Sarah Jane's bird friend

I never did get the IPod. The truth is I do enjoy talking to my plants, our boys and the animals.

By the end of April, the garden was finally looking like a proper vegetable patch. The green peas had crept up and flowered as they reached the first stage of the framework that Nigel had created with the sticks from the barn and some string. The only sacred area at the moment was the sitting area near the bread oven as I was determined to have somewhere to sit in the evenings to write and plan for the days and weeks ahead.

It was currently warmer outside, than it was in the house as we had now moved our living area down to the cave. The cave which had no floor only trodden earth had metre thick stone walls, ideal for keeping the house cool in summer, but in spring when the wood burner was not alight it was pretty cold.

Nigel continues with renovation work

Nigel was working on building and reinforcing the chimney so that we would soon be able to have a proper safe working wood burner when we needed it. At the end of the month as I sat by the brook contemplating the progression of not only the vegetable patch, but the animal enclosures I was feeling very blessed. With the heat of the sun and clear blue skies above me I felt invincible as things were going to plan, and I started to believe in the results to we had to come.

We were planting radishes and lettuces on a three weekly cycle so that we would always have a supply. Trying to work this into the cramped spaces that remained was awkward, to say the least as I had totally underestimated how bushy some of the plants would get. The saving grace was the sweetcorn patch because I had read that you can, and should, plant in-between the sweetcorn. Therefore, as I prepared and planted my sixteen sweetcorn plants I was also now busy planting lettuces in the spaces in-between on the edge. I added carrots to the centre as I knew they would survive in the shade of the tall sweetcorn plants.

The secretly competitive nature of gardening was beginning to show. I was now observing my neighbour's gardens just as they had been observing mine. Nigel frequently told me off for staring when we took the 'boys' past André's garden on their morning and evening walks. However as April drew to a close I received the first sign of my acceptance as a kitchen gardener in France when André invited me into his garden to have a tour of his tomato plants. He then walked with me to our garden where he pointed at my tomato plants which were double the size of his. He made his puzzled rubbing of the chin gesture as I pointed to my buckets of stinging nettle plant food that I used to water my tomatoes with each day. The smell was terrible, but apparently it was a natural way to feed tomato plants and was supposed to help prevent tomato blight. I had my fingers crossed for this being successful.

As I tried to explain that it was stinging nettles in the buckets soaked in water from the brook, I had to pretend to pick one and then rub the skin on my arm as if scratching it. Eventually, I got the thumbs up that he understood me as he scuttled off straight into Yvette's kitchen. He was obviously going to discuss the latest crazy stunt by the English woman next door.

Gardening tip – Stinging nettle plant food (This is NOT for human consumption!!)

Stinging nettles are an easy and free way to make your own plant food. To make your nettle plant food you will need the basic ingredients of stinging nettles which are readily available. If they do not grow in your garden, you will find them along the road-side and footpaths. You will need some buckets; I used the black industrial ones. I wasn't confident that my cheap three euro buckets would contain this purulent mixture over a long period as it smells as if it could corrode anything it comes into contact with including skin!

It's pretty easy just collect your nettles and cut them into short enough lengths so that they lie flat in the bucket, a bit like breaking up spaghetti for boiling. Before putting them into the bucket stamp on them a bit to release the juice from the stems and place them in the bucket and fill it with water. Stir the mixture twice daily and keep pushing down any nettles that float to the surface.

If you struggle to keep them under the water try laying a brick or some stones on them. However, remember what you put in you have to get out. If the mixture touches your skin, it will take a lot of scrubbing to remove the smell.

It takes around four weeks to brew. If possible leave it longer, as it gets better with time, that's why we had buckets at various stages of development around the garden. My top tip, learnt the hard way as usual, always place the buckets as far away as possible from the house or any windows or doors as it tends to get rather smelly. Before using it to water the plants always dilute it in a watering-can. It should resemble cold tea in colour. Be sure not to waste any part of this process. However off-putting it may be, you can put the smelly sludge from the bottom of the bucket into your compost bin. Another good tip is - never use the nettle plant food bucket for anything else, it will always smell of the nettle mixture and instantly contaminates any liquid added.

Chapter 4
May

The chicken enclosure was finished, and the chickens that had suddenly grown over the last three weeks have been safely transferred to their new outdoor living quarters. Nigel positioned branches in the enclosure for roosting, straw for bedding and left a patch of grass, which did not stay grassy for long as it was adjacent to the water bath. Rosie, the rabbit had also now been transferred to the enclosure. A strange combination five chickens and a rabbit, which we initially thought was female but which turned out to be male!! We had researched this new living arrangement on the internet and apparently chickens and rabbits are compatible. Therefore, the rabbit hutch was positioned in one corner and the chicken house in the other, but they had to share the open area. However, that was not the problem we encountered with this arrangement.

The whole enclosure was adjacent to the boy's exercise area; meaning Dave and Buster were continuously jumping up at the fencing barking at the chickens and the rabbit. The arrangement did not bode well for future egg production, so we barricaded the wire fencing with wood from pallets and pieces of cardboard as a temporary measure to block their view although the boys were unrelenting.

Chicken enclosure – top right

By mid-May two of the chickens had started demonstrating what we hoped was imitation cock-a-doodle-dooing. We were surrounded by three roosters at neighbouring properties and internet research reassured us that chickens can imitate rooster noise especially if they do not have a rooster in their enclosure.

We would leave them to it and hope that they lost interest in this annoying pastime. However, it soon became more pronounced, and when they started to be become aggressive when we entered the enclosure we had it confirmed by our French neighbours, two of them at least were cockerels. It was not the way we planned our first attempt at chicken keeping in France.

Ginger Spice is definitely looking like a cockerel

The saga of the chickens and cockerels will be continued.

One morning I opened the back door to start my morning weeding and organic pest control. Armed with my grey water spray and crushed up eggs shells, in my usual clumsy unobservant fashion I fell face first onto a large wooden box filled to overflowing with rhubarb. As I glanced across the garden to Yvette's path, I noticed her rhubarb had gone and deduced that this was it. The box was too heavy for me to lift it into the house, so I wondered how she, a woman of 83, had managed to get it here. Or had she filled it here? If that was the case, why have the boys been so tolerant? It was unlike them to let anyone walk to the back door unannounced. I spend the morning preparing the rhubarb to make into jam as I did not want to waste it even thought this was now an additional task in my already busy gardening schedule. I quickly researched a recipe for making frugal jam and despite the method sounding strange, it was frugal, so I thought I would give it a try.

This method of making jam focused on removing the lengthy stove top cooking time. It turned out to be a lengthy method to complete so even though you don't have the stove on purposefully for making the jam the process is not quick, but it is cheap.

Rhubarb Jam recipe

Ingredients:

2 kg rhubarb

2 kg sugar

Method

Day 1

To prepare the rhubarb firstly cut the big leaves off then chop the rhubarb stalks into pieces approximately 1 cm in size. If the stalk is thick, then cut the pieces smaller. Be sure to use the white part even though it looks like waste as this adds natural sweetness to whatever you are cooking.

Place a layer of rhubarb into a large pan then add a layer of sugar on top, repeat until all of the rhubarb and sugar have been used. Cover and rest the jam saucepan for a few hours or overnight to remove some of the juices from the rhubarb.

Day 2

Yes, it takes days! I am not sure of the origin of this recipe as there are various adaptations of it on the internet. Due to our meagre cooking facilities i.e. we had no kitchen, I had to adapt the recipe for our appliances but the idea of this frugal method is to conserve the electricity needed for the cooking process. The idea was simple enough. Whenever you were cooking i.e. your eggs for breakfast or your vegetables for dinner, you place the rhubarb jam saucepan on the hob that had been used afterwards, thus using the remainder of the heat available while the hob cools down to cook the jam. However, if you have a gas cooker this does not work, but with a wood-burner you can cook this jam in a few hours. Fortunately rhubarb cooks quite quickly. On the first day of cooking, if the heat from your cooling hob does not bring the jam to the boil, you will need to give it a 10 minute boost, stirring continually to prevent it burning on the bottom. Then turn the heat off and leave the jam to rest. The aim is to repeat this twice a day. By this stage, the jam has taken on a deep red colour and thickened.

Remember never to boil vigorously as the sugar may overheat, and the flavour may be affected. When filling the sterilised jars follow general instructions about hygiene.

A tip I learned was to lay cling film on the top of the jam then place an extra layer of sugar on the top to seal it, thus preventing mould formation. The jam can be stored in the cupboard for up to a year, and this recipe made six jars of jam.

The Potatoes are ready!

Our potato growing and harvest was one of our success stories in the summer of 2013. Against the advice of our elderly French neighbours who have been growing potatoes since before we were born we planted our first set of seedlings early before the last frost. Despite this, and due to Nigel's vigilant attention to topping up the mounds around the potato plants, by May we were able to start harvesting and eating our home grown new potatoes. We were totally unprepared for how many potatoes each plant would produce, so we had to become inventive to avoid potato eating boredom.

Sarah Jane's first harvest of new potatoes

Hence, the following recipes came to be:

Cheese and leek jacket potatoes

We cooked these in the bread oven whilst working on the exterior of the house, but it also works well in a conventional oven. This recipe serves 4

Ingredients:

4 large potatoes

1 large leek

2 cloves of garlic

25g butter (or margarine for a more frugal option)

225g cheese grated

Seasoning

Chopped herbs - coriander, rosemary and thyme

Method

Scrub the potatoes and pierce the skin all around with a fork.

Wrap each potato in aluminium foil and place on a heat-stone and slide into the bread oven for one hour approximately, checking their progress after 30 minutes.

For a conventional oven place them directly onto the oven shelf, not on a baking tray, for 40 minutes.

Melt the butter in a frying pan or on a heat-stone from the bread oven and add the chopped leeks, garlic, seasoning, rosemary and thyme. Cook for 5 minutes until the leeks are soft but not brown.

Remove the potatoes from the oven. Cut them in half and scoop out the soft potato and mix it with the leeks and butter mixture and most of the grated cheese.

Refill the potato skins and sprinkle the top with the remaining cheese before replacing in the oven for a further 5-10 minutes to crisp up the top.

These make a delicious lunch or a great supper when served with a green salad and some chutney or relish.

Jaime's recipe for Teenage Wedges

One of the things Jaime missed in France was proper chips; English/Australian chip shop chips. Pomme frites or French fries are thin and often limp and so did not meet her chip criteria. Therefore with a bumper harvest of new potatoes we tried a variation.

Although we couldn't make deep fried chips because being frugal meant we didn't want to commit a large amount of cooking oil to this project, we decided to try our version of baked potato wedges. These were another of her favourite potato dishes.

This recipe serves 3 people.

Ingredients:

6 medium size new potatoes or 4 larger old potatoes

2 tbsp olive oil vegetable oil to grease baking tray

Salt, pepper and dried herbs.

Method

Clean and scrub potatoes do not peel them.

Slice into wedges and place in a bowl of cold water for 10 minutes

Lightly grease a baking tray with vegetable oil, drain the wedges and dry on kitchen towel then empty the water, dry the bowl and return wedges to the bowl.

Add the olive oil, salt and pepper and sprinkle with dried herbs. Gently toss the wedges with a spatula to coat them in the seasoning and oil mix.

Place the wedges evenly on a baking tray, and bake on a medium heat in the oven for 40 minutes, turning after 20 minutes so both sides are brown and crispy. To test, they should be soft in the middle.

Jaime loved making these to have with homemade tomato relish or dips, or they can also be an accompaniment to chops or chicken with green salad. As a lover of the McDonald's breakfast Jaime also made her version of hash browns, here is her recipe.

McJaime Hash Browns

Ingredients

3 tbsp olive oil

25g butter or margarine softened

1 lb. new potatoes

Seasoning

Method

Peel and grate the potatoes. Squeeze out as much moisture as you can from the grated potatoes by placing them in a clean tea towel or between layers of kitchen towels.

Heat 3 tbsp of oil in a large frying pan on medium heat.

Add the butter or margarine to the grated potato mixing them well. Shape the grated potato into golf ball sized patties and gently flatten them before placing them into the frying pan. Season them once they are in the pan.

After a few minutes, flip them over to cook the other side using a spatula. These made a lovely addition to our egg and bacon treat on a Sunday morning if Nigel had worked that week.

One of my potato 'must do's' for the year was that the tiniest ones would be blanched and put into the freezer so that we would eat home-grown new potatoes with our Christmas dinner. I love tiny new potatoes in the summer, but there is something very decadent about eating them in winter. As we harvested our new potatoes, I selected the best quality and size for my freezer project and froze more than I need really, but they are delicious. We were eating them every day boiled with quiche and salad or by making them into potato salad. Sometimes at the weekend any leftover boiled potatoes were sliced, slowly fried in olive oil and garlic and served with a fried egg.

As we had gone overboard on the planting of potatoes, it quickly became apparent that we would need to find other ways to store them for winter use other than as cooked dishes or by freezing them. After some internet research, the answer came in the form of storing them in the wooden pallet boxes on layers of newspaper.

The process is very simple. First, brush off all loose dirt, do not wash them. Check each potato for any sign of infestation, bruising or damage from harvesting. Only perfect potatoes can be stored as even one damaged or rotten potato will ruin the remaining stock. Layer the potatoes in the pallet or box side by side not overlapping. When one layer is full, cover them with newspapers and then layer again. When the pallet or box is full, add a final layer of newspaper.

We then used an old security jacket of Nigel's to wrap up the box to ensure that no light was able to reach the potatoes as this would make them start to produce shoots. We had planned to store the wrapped up boxes in the barn, but we were worried that moisture from the leaking roof may penetrate them, so they ended up in the bedroom with other produce. As the summer went on our bedroom resembled a greengrocer's store room!

Chapter 5
June

Sarah Jane's fresh garden peas

As the sun continued to shine, and June arrived, while harvesting my peas I was informed by André and Yvette that my haricot verte (green beans) should be in the ground by now. After months of me being the first to plant and harvest crops, I was now the one who was behind schedule. How did that happen? And why must I call them haricot verte even though they are green beans? Apparently it's just the way it is here in France, I can call all the other vegetables by their English names but not these beans. I wondered if this had something to do with the numerous varieties of beans, as I remembered as a child that my grandmother always called them French runner beans.

On Yvette's daily inspections of my vegetable patch, she admired my flags that marked and named the rows. For some of the plants, which she recommended, I translated my English labelling into French for which she would give me the thumbs up if it was correct. This was indeed an honour because Yvette speaks 'patois' or old French which is thought to originate from rural regional dialects. I wasn't sure if there was a special way to write this as I couldn't find any guidance on it. Either way she obviously understood the words. At last I was making some progress with the language, even if it was only in writing it!

The second planting of leeks took place in the area where some of the lettuces had been. The soil is getting richer and improving in drainage with each planting of the various above and below ground crops. On the 10th June, we harvested the first crop of beetroot.

I deliberately harvested them while they were small to medium sized as I didn't want to risk them developing a flavourless, woody texture as I intended to pickle them. We have always enjoyed baby beetroot which are delicious with salads or sandwiches any time of year therefore I was eager to preserve as many as possible.

Pickling beetroot the frugal way.

Ingredients:

Beetroot

Brown vinegar

Method:

Harvest the beetroot and remove all loose soil. Cut off the leaves off about 2 inches away from the beetroot, don't cut them any closer or the beetroot will bleed during the boiling process and turn white. Do not discard the leaves as they are delicious cooked/wilted like spinach and served as a vegetable dish or they can be used like spinach in recipes such as frittata.

Boil the beetroot until the skins can be rubbed away. Depending on the size it can take 40-50 minutes to reach this stage.

Drain the beetroot and place in cold water.

Rub away the skin and the root and 2 inch stalk. This cooked waste product from the beetroot was devoured by our chickens, but if you don't have chickens, it can go into the compost bin.

Slice or place the whole baby beetroots into sterilised jars and cover with brown vinegar. Cover with air tight lid, label and store for up to one year. Over the summer, we made 32 jars of pickled beetroot.

Courgettes ready to flower

This week also saw the first courgette flowers form and appear, as if synchronized, they flowered from one end of the row to the other in a perfectly ordered sequence. Is that Mother Nature declaring their readiness or just coincidence? In Australia, we became regular consumers of courgette flowers sautéed in garlic. As we were now in France with copious amounts of home-grown garlic, there was no excuse not to indulge in this delicacy which makes a good looking and tasty starter for dinner parties

Garlic and herb sautéed courgette flowers

Ingredients

12 freshly opened courgette flowers, with the stamens removed.

3 cloves of garlic

Chopped Italian parsley

Coriander leaves

Olive oil

Method

In a frying pan heat the olive oil slowly, and then carefully spoon in the washed courgette flowers.

Stir gently as the flowers wilt, which only takes about 1-2 minutes.

Combine the grated garlic, chopped parsley and coriander and add it to the frying pan, carefully turning the mixture with a spatula. If it starts to look dry, then drizzle over a little extra olive oil. Season to taste.

This dish is usually served as a starter on a bed of rocket or small spinach leaves. Delicious!

Preparing for storage

We were eating garlic and onions daily from the garden. However, the task of preparing the surplus for storage for use over the winter needed to begin in earnest as we had a bumper crop to process.

Garlic

Over the years, I have often seen photographs in magazines and on the internet of the iconic French garlic plait. However, to date I had only bought garlic from the supermarket. They often hang a plastic replica of a garlic plait in the greengrocery area to entice you to buy the garlic or other French produce even though a lot of supermarket garlic actually originates from Spain or China. I had never seen garlic growing, and so I had no idea how the tail-like foliage that the garlic plant produces would be used in the plaiting process. As we planted our garlic in February, by June, the plants were knee height and so we researched how to know when the garlic was ready for harvesting and storing.

The instructions were as follows:

"Wait for the leaves to start to turn brown and fold/fall over. When this happens, it is advisable to stop watering as this helps with the curing process."

However, it was sods law, as they say that it rained for two days solid as soon as our garlic was ready. Secondly, contrary to the way the French people do it, our research indicated that it was best to dig up your garlic rather than pulling it from the ground. The reason is that the foliage will snap leaving the bulb in the ground, thus making it unsuitable to be stored. Garlic plants develop deep roots during the growing season therefore we used a garden fork just like digging new potatoes. Once they have been dug it is important to leave the stalks and roots on and just brush away the soil.

We laid ours in wooden pallets to dry initially in the sunshine until Yvette shouted, "Non" and pointed to the barn and then to the wooden pallet, indicating that I needed to move them immediately. I later read that exposure to direct sunlight can change the flavour of the garlic. Once they were dried we brushed them again to remove any remaining soil. It is important to take them indoors or put them in a dry area for this drying and curing process.

After three weeks, the stalks and roots were brown and dead. The roots can be gently rubbed off or trimmed if they are persistent. If you want to plait them then leave the stalks on.

When the girls were young, I used to plait their hair every morning for school just as my mum had done for me when I was a child. Therefore, I did not anticipate any issues with plaiting some dried stalks of garlic. Naive? Most definitely. I sat on my fluorescent green plastic chair in the garden with my box of garlic. I knew what I wanted it to look like, but my mind was completely blank as to how to achieve the layered garlic look with no straggling stalks. After a few failed attempts, I resorted to some internet research. I read and reread the instructions that reminded me of reading a Haynes car mechanic manual; it made no sense to me at all without the pictures. So after some further research I found a YouTube video and then I was ready.

I will try to explain the process. In very basic terms you take the three largest bulbs and lay them on a flat surface, you plait the three stems as you would hair to about one inch in length. Take a new bulb and lay it in the centre beneath the middle bulb and add its stalk to the plaiting. Plait again for one turn then add a new bulb to the right, plait again then add a bulb to the left and continue. And so it continues adding one bulb at a time centre, right then left keeping the braid tight. If any of the stalks snap then a simple trick is it to tie a piece of garden string around the plait above the break. Then tie it to the broken off stalk and then continue to plait incorporating the end of the string to keep it looking tidy yet secure. It sounds quite horrendous when you try to write or explain it, but in reality it's quite easy once you get started.

Once the garlic bulbs are plaited they need to hang in a well-ventilated area. However do not hang them in the kitchen because of the excessive moisture and heat which will damage them. I hung ours on the landing on the unused fireplace over winter and then in spring I moved them to outside the back door in our covered porch area. The garlic was fabulous, and they lasted throughout the winter. From the whole 39 bulbs, we had only one clove with mould which I think is pretty good.

My first garlic plait of 2013

Onions

Now when it came to storing the onions after harvest that was a whole different ball game. Although you can plait them like the garlic, our onions were so big and heavy I doubted if I had string or a nail strong enough to hang them from afterwards. Therefore, we went for the box method. So, just as we did with the garlic, the first stage was to harvest with a fork and then dry and brush them. This time when they have been drying for three weeks you brush off or trim the roots and cut the stalks about 1 inch from the bulb. The skins will have started to go tight and over the coming weeks they will darken and go shiny. I placed my curing onions in wooden fruit pallets from the supermarket lined with newspaper. A tip I learnt after the first week of curing, check all the onions carefully for signs of damage or rotting because if you get a rotten bulb it will disintegrate and become a liquid producing ball. If this happened, you would need to remove it and the fluid it produced without changing the whole box as the onions do not like being disturbed during the curing process. I think I would like to be an onion undisturbed over winter.

Now curing the onions needs to be done in the dark so initially I laid newspapers above and below and placed a coat over them. The advantage of using the wooden fruit pallets was also that they were made to be stacked which is good because we had five boxes of onions. At week six, after checking the onions each week and discarding, or using, any that still had green stems or looked to be going soft, the next task was to individually wrap each one in newspaper ready to store. A daunting task to start with but one which became quite therapeutic when you sit there thinking of all the food you are squirrelling away for the winter.

As usual due to the temperature and ventilation requirements, these boxes also ended up in the bedroom, another good reason for not wanting any rotten ones in the pallets.

Elderflowers

By the 16th June, the elderflowers were now hanging heavy with white flowers. The unmistakable scent, strong and to some people off-putting, in no way resembles the flavour of anything made from the flowers. The elderflowers that had until now been just small buds were now white flowers and as instructed by André ready for eating! I have never eaten an elderflower, although I have eaten flowers before as Sheila, Nigel's mum, used to add nasturtiums to salads. However, elderflower heads always looked too much like a weed for my liking, and I wasn't keen on the scent either. Despite this, the flowers were collected as we walked the boys, and we researched and began our first attempt at making a cordial from elderflowers.

Elderflower Cordial

Ingredients:

30-40 large Elderflower heads,

1kg sugar

1.5 litres boiling water

3 large lemons

50g citric acid- tablet or powder form (available from winemaking department in supermarkets or local pharmacy) we had ours sent over from the UK.

Method

Clean the elderflowers by gently shaking them under slow running water, to remove dirt, debris and possible insects.

Place the sugar into a large saucepan and add the boiling water, stirring until dissolved. Place to one side to cool.

Using a fine grater, grate the lemons and stir them into the sugar water. Stir in the citric acid then cut the lemons into slices and add to the mixture.

Place the elderflowers into the mixture stirring gently.

The mixture now needs to stand for two days, covered and protected from the extreme of heat or cold.

After two days the elderflowers have steeped, like tea-leaves, and the mixture can be strained through a muslin cloth into a clean container. I have a confession to make here. I didn't have muslin, and I had no idea where to buy it, so I used a piece of my cross stitch canvas, which worked well. The canvas would be used as a pouch for bouquet-garni and to add spices to the mulled wine later in the year, but that's another story,

Using a funnel, or in our case the top of a plastic lemonade bottle cut off, fill the sterilized bottles. Once sealed and labelled the bottles need to be stored in a cool, dark place for at least a month.

This refreshing cordial is delicious when diluted with sparkling water and ice. It can also be used as flavouring in cakes and puddings.

Wild cherries

We have been watching the cherry trees on our daily dog walks and over the last few weeks even before we knew they were cherries we marvelled at the abundance of berries forming. When they suddenly adopted the iconic long stem and dark maroon cherry image we couldn't resist tasting them. The sweetness was extreme and had we been ready or confident of our decision we would have picked a plentiful supply. However, in our hesitation, by the following day when we did go prepared to harvest some of them they were gone. Obviously someone else in the village recognised them and was now enjoying a bountiful harvest. Maybe next year.

Can I grow peanuts in France?

This may seem like a strange question, but on the 18th June after finding a solitary peanut tree plant in the garden centre reduced to one euro this experiment had to be undertaken. We planted the peanut tree in a small area near to the boundary adjacent to Yvette's garden. We surrounded it with slate tiles from the roof to protect it from being trodden on accidentally by Yvette on her way over to view our garden each morning. In my crude translation of the growing instructions, it said we would have peanuts in 120 days. I marked it in my diary and started to count the days as I observed its unremarkable growth. Watch this space for peanut news!

Chapter 6
July

Jaime left home in June to study in the UK and, as July arrived, Nigel was away competing in the Para's 10 endurance race. Wouldn't you know it that emergency butchery needed to be done on our little farmstead? Unfortunately, I couldn't wait for Nigel to return to help me; even though he doesn't do any of the killings he would catch the birds for me. Yvette was becoming annoyed, possibly distressed, it's hard to tell which, by the horrendous noise of four cockerels in close proximity to her garden. I found myself hiding in the barn when she came outside to harvest her lettuce, etc., for lunch, because she looks across at the chicken enclosure, shakes her fist and mutters to herself in French. When I dared to come out, I could see her sitting near her back door covering her ears. It was time for something to be done before I got into trouble with the Maire for creating a noise nuisance. In France anyone with a problem in the village goes to the Maire, and he sorts it out. This is usually done by sending someone to knock on your door, tell you in French what you have been accused of doing and instructing you to rectify it immediately. Fortunately, it hasn't happened to us yet, but I know some of the English people in the village have been 'warned' over certain issues. The aim, therefore, is to not disrespect the rules of the village.

The 7th July sees the culling begin in our little livestock division. The five chickens have turned into one chicken and four cockerels, and our brood has shattered the peace of this quiet idyll. The angst and testosterone in the enclosure between the male rabbit and the now assertive cockerels reached fever point when Rosie the rabbit mounted one of the cockerels as his hormones obviously got the better of him. The cockerel let him know in no uncertain terms that his back and any other body parts were off limits, and so the pecking wars began. However, Rosie was not slow to retaliate and proceeded to bite at his legs quite successfully which then resulted in a standoff. Something had to be done.

Angry birds!

    I decided somewhat unwisely that the most aggressive cockerel, Scary Spice, who was later renamed Miranda as she/he appeared large and clumsy like the TV comedienne of the same name, would be first. I prepared the utility area for the slaughter, plucking and gutting and went to the chicken enclosure. Strangely enough because of the birds clumsiness the catching element was uneventful. However, as I exited the enclosure Yvette saw me and laughed with a thumbs up. She obviously guessed what was going on, and I think I gained some kudos for finally deciding to slaughter a bird instead of fussing around them. In the utility area, the gruesome task was completed. As my punishment, I received a wing across my face which startled and shocked me enough to allow the claws of one foot to escape my grip and penetrate my forearm drawing blood. What an awful experience while home alone. I went indoors to sort out my injuries before deciding one was enough while Nigel was away whatever the noise consequences might be.

Nigel's homecoming meal

Chicken, however I used a cockerel, one pot meal.

Ingredients:

Whole chicken or chicken pieces

1 onion or leek

8 whole small new potatoes

1 large carrot

4 large florets of broccoli

1 pint chicken stock

For the budget herby dumplings:

Suet and butter are expensive luxuries when you are on a tight food budget, so I replaced that element of the recipe by using grated cooking margarine which is only 59 cents a packet.

250 g self-raising flour

125g hard margarine

Cold water

Seasoning

Mixed herbs fresh or dried

Method:

Place the chicken in an oven-proof dish which either has a lid or can be covered with aluminium foil. Pour in the stock and add the chopped onion or leek, and carrots. Put it in the oven for 40 minutes.

While the chicken is cooking prepare the herby dumplings by placing the flour in a bowl and adding the grated hard margarine. Stir the mixture, season and sprinkle in the herbs. Start to add the cold water, a little at a time while stirring slowly until a sticky dough forms. Roll the dough into small balls, approximately golf ball sized, and place onto a floured plate.

Remove the dish from the oven and place the broccoli florets, whole uncooked potatoes and dumplings around the chicken.

Season, cover and cook for a further 20-30 minutes or until potatoes are soft, and the dumplings are cooked through.

This dish can be served alone or with some freshly steamed peas or beans, making a hearty meal after a hard day of renovating or gardening

Nigel returned, and immediately things were being moved around, he is a Virgo and very particular about a place for everything and everything in its place. While he had been away, I had used what I wanted, placed it where I wanted it or sometimes I even misplaced things. I was in trouble now as I hadn't replaced some of his tools that I had used for alternative purposes in his absence. For example, the Phillip's screwdriver I had used to make holes in a piece of cross stitch canvas didn't go down well as I had left threads entwined on the screwdriver.

However, the day after his return I went outside to hang out the washing on our make-shift washing line. The line runs the length of the garden secured on the barn and a big alder tree near the brook however it sagged in the middle due to its length. I started hanging the washing out and reached for my prop which I always leave leaning against the grave vine trellis. It was not there. I looked around thinking it must have fallen over, but there was no sign of it. I looked across the garden, and I could see Nigel with his head down, but obviously chuckling to himself. '

"Ok, where is it?" I wondered, thinking he was playing a practical joke on me.

Then looking serious again he says "I forgot it was the prop, so I used it."

"How can you forget it's a prop; a long piece of wood with V-shaped top? What on earth did you need that for?"

He didn't say anything he just looked across at the grape vine which was fully laden with green grapes and trailing across the barn wall. My eyes followed his and then I spotted it.

"You've cut it up?"

"I can't let the grapes touch the ground and the netting needs to stay in place to keep the birds off. That's next year's wine hanging there!"

"So my washing can touch the ground instead, great!"

Grape growing in progress

In fairness to Nigel, he did go out that afternoon and find a new branch to make a new prop, and I was immediately forgiven for not returning things to their proper places.

Tomato disaster

As readers of 'Two dogs and a suitcase' will know our tomato plants suffered from blight despite the application of our organic nettle plant food. They were heavy with green tomatoes which were unaffected, so we harvested them and made chutney. It took several batches of chutney to make use of them all. However, on the last batch the gas bottle for the stove ran out and with nowhere open to get a refill we had to light the wood burner to finish cooking it by placing it on the top. You do not need the wood burner alight in July when the temperature is sitting between 25 – 35 degrees Celsius, but I was determined that no chutney would be wasted. News of my tomato disaster had obviously spread because that afternoon when we walked the boys the three wise French elders, Yvette, Janine and André, were waiting for me. They indicated that Nigel needed to take the boys home as they took my arm and led me to their outdoor kitchen. Inside they presented me with a box of tomato plants and instructions in French. I think the look on my face at the sight of the instructions was a giveaway because the next thing I knew Janine had pulled out the English to French dictionary from her apron pocket. We then sat down as they helped me to translate the instructions, with André doing his customary thumbs up when I indicated my understanding of their instructions. The plants were all healthy looking specimens, about 12 inches in height. They explain in gestures, with the addition of my pigeon French, that they must not be planted anywhere near the site where my blight infected tomatoes had been. I took them home and decided that, as the blight tomatoes had been near the barn, these precious specimens would be planted down near the courgettes and beetroot as everything down there was thriving. I was honoured to be helped by the Chirac, French gardening fraternity and entrusted with plants cultivated with many years of experience. Obviously they would visit daily to make sure I tended to them correctly.

Fortunately, we were still harvesting good crops of new potatoes which we dug fresh every day, for our needs. Nigel could not live on potatoes and vegetables alone so towards the end of the month it was time to use up odds and end in the fridge.

Budget Leftovers Meal

Ingredients:

2 sausages,

2 rashers bacon

Tin of chickpeas

½ tin plum tomatoes

1 tsp chilli powder mix

Method.

Brown the sausages to seal them. Remove from pan and chop into inch size pieces. Cut up the bacon and lay it with the sausage pieces in an oven proof dish. Drain then add the tinned chickpeas and stir in the chilli powder. Cover the top with leftover sliced new potatoes and sprinkle with cheese and herbs. Place in the oven for 20 minutes then serve.

It's jam making time.

The hedgerows are filled with blackberries, and the Australian lady living in a restoration project in the village had introduced us to the French practice of gleaning or 'le glaneur'. Basically, it is the word to describe the gathering of leftover fruit and vegetables from local farmers' after they have harvested. The French believe this practice was an early attempt at providing welfare to the needy.

We were not brave enough to enter farmers' fields, even after being reassured that we could. However, as a result of our local gleaning from verges and pathways around fields, which still felt wrong, as if we were stealing, we had acquired blackberries, greengages, plums and apples.

The gleaned plums made six jars of jam with this recipe.

Plum Jam

Ingredients:

1kg of ripe wild plums

1 kg of white granulated sugar

½ pint/275ml of water

Method:

Thoroughly check and wash the plums, throwing away any damaged or insect eaten plums. In a large saucepan put in the plums and the water and simmer gently until they are soft and the skins split. Add the sugar to the fruit, stirring gently on a low heat until all of the sugar is dissolved. Turn up the heat, keep stirring and let the fruit boil for 10 minutes. Stir through with a sieve spoon to remove the stones during this boiling period.

The easiest way to check if the jam is ready is a simple method given to me by my friend Jackie. Place an empty plate or saucer in the fridge for 10 minutes. Drizzle a teaspoonful of warm jam onto the cold plate, and then return the plate to the fridge to cool for two minutes. If the jam is ready, when you run your finger through it you will crack the jam surface like thin ice on a puddle. If after two minutes the cooled jam is too liquid, continue to boil the jam, testing it every few minutes until you achieve the right result. Always sterilise the jars before potting up the jam.

When potting up the jam allow the jam to settle before applying the cling film or grease-proof paper and a screw top lid. Label when cool and store in a cool, dark place.

The greengage jam was made substituting plums with greengages and using the plum recipe.

Blackberry Jam

Ingredients:

1 kg blackberries

1kg sugar

2 tbs lemon juice

Method:

In a large saucepan or preserving pot place the blackberries and half a pint of water, bring to the boil before adding the sugar and lemon juice. On a medium heat continue cooking at boiling point for 10 minutes, stirring continuously.

Pour the jam into sterilised jars and seal. Once the jam is open and in use it needs to be stored in the fridge.

Nigel's Home-brew

The gleaning of small hard apples resulted in the homebrew cider getting under way. The apples were sour because it was not quite apple time, but they were falling after a recent storm. One of the gleaning tips is to take from the ground the day you see them fall, so we did. As usual improvisation was required when it came to needing brewer's yeast. Therefore, Nigel used my bread making yeast, the least expensive option.

Chirac Cider

Here's the basic process:

6.5kg apples

2 x 7g of bread making yeast

600g sugar

7 pints water

Collect the windfall apples discarding those with maggot entry points or that have been pecked at by birds.

Wash the apples and dry them with a clean towel checking them again for insects. For this recipe, the apples are not peeled.

Cut the apples into quarters and remove the cores and any evidence of bruising. Place the quarters into freezer bags suck the air out with a straw and then keep in the freezer for 48 hours.

Cider making is best performed with a large bucket with a lid.

Pour in seven pints of cold water before adding the apples and the sugar. Sprinkle in the yeast and stir well. Be careful where you place the bucket. Although we have wood and concrete floors indoors we placed it on a newspaper because a lot of condensation formed on the outside of the bucket and dripped down.

We wanted to make about a gallon of cider so we had pre-marked the bucket to indicate one gallon because we had read that the fluid level will need topping up throughout the process. The contents of the bucket need to be stirred well once a day. By day four, bubbling should have commenced as the yeast gets to work. If it hasn't you may have placed the bucket in an area that is too cold, the yeast likes a warm but not hot environment. After a week, you can taste the mixture.

If the apple taste is not strong enough, you can add more apples; they don't have to be the same variety.

Over the coming week, you need to continue to stir on alternate days. At two weeks when you taste it you will notice it has a drier taste now. You can add a bit more sugar, to reactivate the mixture and keep the activity going. It is important to check the inside of the bucket lid daily and clean it as required as the sweet mixture is an ideal breeding ground for bacteria.

After three weeks of stirring, tasting and making small additions of water, maybe apples and extra sugar to get the taste you like, the content will become more liquid as the sediment sinks to the bottom. Without stirring you need to by hand remove the sediment by hand. I wore a new pair of washing up gloves for hygiene purposes. Don't be too fussy just lift out the majority, you don't want the lid off for too long.

Let the liquid settle for 24 hours before tasting again. If the taste is how you like it then it's time to pour it into a demijohn or mini glass barrels like scrumpy bottles. After the activity of being transferred, a froth will form. Wait for it to settle before you put the lid on or air lock if you have one. If the level in the bottle goes down you can top up with water or apple juice.

After a few days, most of the sediment will have dropped. At this stage because we had used large glass bottles from the local Emmaus charity store we decide not to decant into smaller bottles, but to leave it. However, you can decant now to separate the cider from the remaining sediment. When transferring to smaller bottles, it is advisable to leave an inch gap at the top for any activity that restarts. Keep your bottles upright.

We tasted our cider two weeks later, and it certainly packed a punch, so we decided to leave it for Christmas. A top tip for adding some extra fizz is to add a teaspoon of sugar to each bottle. However, make sure the bottle is not overfilled so that the cider has room to expand or the lids will pop off.

Courgettes

The courgettes were turning into large marrows, and we needed to use them quickly. Nigel didn't need telling twice as he got to work on another homebrew project.

Courgette wine

Ingredients:

Courgettes/Marrows - 6 lbs

Sugar - 3 lbs (Recipe stated demerara but is more expensive so we used granulated white sugar)

Root ginger - 1 ounce

Juice of 3 lemons

Yeast

Water

Method:

Wash the marrow and cut it all up. Include the peel, seeds and flesh.

Add it to the crushed ginger root and pour on the boiling water.

Infuse for six days, pressing and stirring daily. Strain and put into a demijohn with the sugar, juice and yeast, and ferment till it stops bubbling (leave for about six months), before bottling.

This makes a delicious white wine which rivals any good chardonnay.

Chapter 7
August

The courgette glut continued, and it forced me to step outside my culinary comfort zone and branch off into cake making. Yes, you read that correctly, cake making. Why is that so strange? Well for those of you who don't know about Nigel and his healthy eating habits, he rarely eats sweet foods of any description due to his fitness regimes and marathon training. It was also due to his childhood payback for eating multiple half penny Blackjack sweets which resulted in numerous dental fillings. My home-made snacks for him to date have centred on my cheesy Chirac scones. The most adventurous, sweet tasting experience he had risked was a spoonful of my homemade jam in his porridge on work days. He also tried a fig biscuit, made from a batch of free figs that he scavenged from a renovation site near Tim's. As promised in my last book, here is the fig biscuit recipe.

Fig biscuits

Ingredients:

For the Short crust pastry

225g plain flour

100g butter or margarine

Pinch salt

For the filling

Figs

1 tbs honey

2 tsp olive oil

300ml water

Method

Make your short crust pastry using this method:

Sieve the flour into a bowl.

Add the butter or margarine, rub it between your fingertips until the mixture resembles fine breadcrumbs.

Stir in the salt, then add 2-3 tbsp water and mix to a firm dough.

Knead the dough briefly and gently on a floured surface.

Wrap in cling film and chill while preparing the filling.

Make your filling:

In a saucepan place your fresh figs, honey and water and bring to the boil. Continue to simmer until it resembles a jam consistency then remove the saucepan from the heat.

Roll out the pastry and cut into rectangles

Along one side of the pastry, spread the fig mixture generously then roll the pastry length-ways (like a Swiss roll.)

Cut the long roll into segments approximately 2-3 inches long. Brush the tops with olive oil before placing them on a baking tray and cooking in a medium oven for about 25 minutes or until the pastry is cooked.

Now back to the courgette cake. The idea of a full blown cake would, and did, initially frighten Nigel, but it was a 'needs must' situation. It was food; it was cheap and we had so many courgettes that we couldn't even give them away because everyone was enjoying a bumper harvest that year.

Courgette cake

Ingredients:

60g raisins

250g courgette grated

2 eggs

125mls olive oil

150g sugar

225g plain flour

½ tsp bicarbonate of soda

½ tsp baking powder

    We could never work out how to get baking powder at Super U, our nearest supermarket, so I omitted that ingredient with no adverse effects. Over the following weeks, I made at least two of these cakes each week to eat or to store in the freezer. We experimented with variations such as adding grated chocolate and red chillies which was Nigel's favourite of my unlikely combinations. Needless to say, the courgette cake with liquorice is a recipe that will go with me to my grave as even the ducks would not entertain tasting it!

Method

Grate the courgette and place it in a colander over a bowl to let excess fluid drain. Cover with a tea-towel and leave for 45 minutes.

Soak the raisins in warm water for 20 minutes to plump them up.

Mix the sugar, eggs and olive oil together, Add the bicarbonate of soda and baking powder to the plain flour before sifting it into the mixture. With a wooden spoon or spatula gently stir in the raisins and then the grated courgette. If you are making a variation like adding chocolate or chillies add them now.

Pour the mixture into a well-greased cake tin or loaf tin and bake on medium heat for about 30 minutes. Test with a sharp knife in the centre, a clean knife means it's ready. Turn it out onto a cooling tray. This is delicious eaten warm and cold. The cake will keep fresh for a week in an airtight container. This cake freezes really well and makes an ideal snack for lunch boxes.

As the end of August approached we had moved from small to medium size courgettes to large marrows. It was time to try some alternative ways of preserving and for Nigel to try his mum's recipe for homemade marrow rum!

Curried courgette chutney

Ingredients:

1 kg courgette chopped

2 tbs salt

2 medium sized onions

5 cloves of garlic

1 red chilli

25 g root ginger

100ml olive oil

25 g root ginger

2 tbs mustard seed

1 tbs coriander

1 tbs turmeric

300ml of brown vinegar

225 mg white sugar

Obviously, in my budget store cupboard some of these items were missing, such as root ginger, turmeric and mustard seeds. Therefore, I improvised with 1 teaspoon of French mustard and a teaspoon of curry powder which gave it a delicious twist.

Method

Wipe the courgette skin and cut off the stalks. Chop into pieces 5 inch long then slice length ways to form ribbons. Place in a colander and rest them over a bowl for 2 hours covered with a tea towel.

Peel the onion garlic and chop the chilli. Mix these into a paste with the mustard, curry powder and half of the olive oil. (If you are using the root ginger, turmeric and mustard seeds use these here.)

Rinse the courgette and pat dry with a clean tea towel or paper towels.

Heat the remainder of the olive oil in a saucepan add the onion and garlic paste and cook for 5 minutes before adding the courgettes, vinegar and sugar.

Stir well and simmer on a low heat for 15 minutes, stirring to ensure that it does not stick to the bottom of the pan.

Pot into sterilised jars while still hot and press down before sealing, I used a layer of cling film with four sugar cubes to weigh it down before applying the lid.

Sheila's Homemade Marrow rum

Now I know the idea sounds bizarre, and I was highly skeptical about the amount of sugar we had to buy on the promise of producing some rum. Rum is a spirit that I had not tasted since my student nurse days when we drank rum and coke on pay-day. Therefore, my memories of rum were not entirely favourable ones, as I did recall a lot of hangovers. Despite this, Nigel was on a mission this summer to make his own wine, rum and cider and this was part of that plan so I went along for the ride as the willing assistant, and trust me it needed an assistant, these marrows were heavy and awkward to manipulate.

Ingredients:

A large ripe marrow with hard skin

5lbs sugar

2 X 7g sachets of bread yeast

Cup of lemon or orange juice

Method:

Using the biggest marrow(s) you have, cut off the stalk end, about 2 inches down, with a saw or large sharp knife. It can be tough, so the best way is to lay it down. You will make the stalk piece that you cut off the lid, so don't break it or throw it away. Scoop out the seeds and pith. It's a messy job, but the ducks loved the marrow contents.

Pack the cavity with the sugar. If you don't have a willing assistant to hold the marrow while you pack it, try putting it into a drawer then gently closing it like a vice to secure it. Or place it in a sturdy plant pot or vase for support.

Mix the yeast with the lemon or orange juice and pour it into the marrow onto the sugar. Replace the lid of the marrow, and seal with tape. We used masking tape. Hang the marrow in a cotton pillow case, with the top pointing upwards, in a warm area. Beware though; as the process gets underway the marrow shell will start to leak, usually at 2-3 weeks.

At this stage, you can make a hole in the bottom of the marrow and drain off the rum liquid into demi-johns or bottles. We strained ours through the cotton pillow case to catch any marrow pieces that had not liquefied during the fermentation process.

    Once bottled the idea is that the longer you can keep this the better it will taste. We made an average of two bottles from each large marrow. Making Nigel wait to sample it did prove tricky, but out of sight is out of mind, so I put it in the barn. This was a big mistake because I forgot where the next stage of the renovation was; yes you guessed it, in the barn where he was building my utility room. The rum had to return indoors and sat looking at him from the top of the dresser in the kitchen. How long did it last? Christmas.

The other vegetable that seemed to show no sign of dying down was the spinach. Although we struggled in the early stages of growing the spinach due to the slugs, once the remaining plants took hold they were prolific, and of course the more you picked, the more you got. The good thing about spinach is that it shrinks enormously during cooking which makes it convenient to freeze as it takes up less space.

Here are a couple of recipes to use the spinach other than as a vegetable as part of the main course.

Spinach and leek omelette

Ingredients:

2 eggs

1 tbsp cold water

Seasoning

1 tsp olive oil

2 tomatoes sliced

1 small leek

4 tbs of wilted spinach or beetroot leaves (wilt by placing it in a sieve and pouring boiling water over it)

Fresh coriander roughly chopped

Grated cheese optional

Method

Whisk the eggs with the water in a bowl and season.

Heat the olive oil in the frying pan and sauté the leeks. When the leeks are soft take the frying pan off the heat and put the wilted spinach on top of the leeks.

Place this leek and spinach mix onto a plate.

Pour some olive oil into the already used frying pan and heat the olive oil gently before pouring the egg mixture in. As the egg starts to solidify return the leeks and spinach to the frying pan and place the sliced tomatoes on top, seasoning again to taste.

Now you can either cook this slowly without turning it, (technically a frittata, I was informed by my well-travelled son Rob,) or you can fold and turn it, cooking for a further 3- 5 minutes. Nigel liked the folded method as he added some grated cheese onto the omelette before I folded it.

Place the cooked omelette on a plate and garnish with the roughly chopped coriander. I served this filling omelette as a delicious lunch served with a green salad.

Bacon and spinach frittata

Ingredients:

1 tbs olive oil

I onion chopped (I used leeks)

1 clove garlic

3 rashers bacon grilled then cut into strips

250 g wilted spinach or beetroot leaves

4 eggs

2 tbsp cheese grated

3 boiled and sliced potatoes

Seasoning

Herbs

Method

Heat the oil in a frying pan without a plastic handle and soften the onion and garlic then add the bacon.

Roughly cut the wilted spinach and add to the pan. Beat the eggs in a bowl and add the grated cheese.

Pour the mixture onto the onion, garlic and bacon.

Add the potato slices on top and sprinkle some more cheese or feta on the top. Sprinkle with herbs and a drizzle of olive oil and slide the pan excluding the handle under the grill for 5 to 7 minutes or until the egg mix is cooked.

Garnish with fresh herbs, I used Italian parsley for this dish which makes another great lunch idea for two people, or as a main meal when served with seasonal fresh vegetables or a salad.

Luxury Fish Pie with rösti topping -Serves 4

Ingredients:

For the fish mixture:

4 fillets of white fish fresh or frozen

5 fl oz (150 ml) dry white wine

1 bay leaf

2 oz (50 g) butter or margarine

2 oz (50 g) plain flour

½ pint milk

1 tbs chopped fresh parsley

1 tbs chopped fresh coriander

Seasoning

For the rösti topping:

1 lb new potatoes

2 oz (50 g) butter, melted

2 oz (50 g) cheese, grated

Method

Clean the potatoes by scrubbing them, but leave the skins on. Grate them onto a plate.

Make a roux for the white sauce by melting the butter or margarine in a saucepan before adding the flour to make a paste. Whisk in the milk and heat it slowly whisking all the time.

(A roux is a cooked mixture of butter or margarine and flour used to thicken sauces, soups, etc.)

When the sauce is hot, add the wine and a bay leaf. Season to taste. Remove from the heat.

Take your four fillets of white fish and crumble them into a well-greased baking dish. Remove the bay leaf and pour the white wine sauce over the fish. Sprinkle with herbs

For the rösti topping, place the grated potato into a bowl and pour over some melted butter, lightly toss the potatoes through the butter to coat it. Spoon the rösti topping onto the fish in sauce and spread gently, but do not push it down. Sprinkle the top with cheese and cook on a medium heat for 35-40 minutes.

Chapter 8
September

As the end of the summer approached, I had accumulated an extensive range of herbs. They included Italian parsley, coriander, thyme, rosemary and mint. Some were still growing well in pots, or in the herb garden, and others were in the process of drying in the house or the barn. I decided to experiment with something that I had read about in a free cooking supplement from Tesco's. The herbs that I could not dry for use over the winter could be stored in olive oil in the freezer in ice cube trays. I had used this method with the wild chives we found back in February, and they were working well, so I decided for this experiment to try sage, thyme and rosemary. The ice cube tray selection of herbs can be bagged up and kept ready for use when sautéing vegetables or to add to dishes before cooking. I wasn't confident about preserving my excess basil this way, so I made it into pesto and froze it in yoghurt pots. When you are growing and using herbs on a budget, you need to ensure you get the full impact of the flavour and maximise the use of the plant.

Home grown herbs whether started from seed or plants from the garden centre or nursery add such depth to the flavour of many dishes and can transform leftovers into a culinary delight. I remember one of my favourites from my childhood was bubble and squeak. It was always served on a Monday using the Sunday roast leftovers. The downside was that it always appeared to have cabbage in it. As a child, I disliked cabbage with a passion whereas now I eat and enjoy all types of cabbage, be it red, white or savoy. My improvised version of bubble squeak was enhanced by the addition of rosemary and thyme. It had no cabbage because our cabbages were eaten by caterpillars despite our intensive organic pest control activities.

Bubble and squeak like mum used to make.

Leftover ingredients:

Mashed, roast or boiled potatoes

Vegetables - leeks, runner beans, carrots, peas, etc.

Meat pieces - cut into small cubes for quick and thorough reheating (meat is optional)

Three sprigs of fresh rosemary

1 clove garlic

1 tablespoon of thyme – with stalks removed

4 tbsp butter

½ cup onion, finely chopped

Black pepper seasoning

Method

Melt the butter in a frying pan and add the chopped onion and garlic. Fry gently until soft not brown. Add the meat pieces, if you are using them, and ensure they are heated through before moving on to the next stage.

Add the potato and vegetables and fry for about 10 minutes or until the potatoes and vegetable are heated through. Turn the mixture with a spatula in the melted butter two or three times.

Press the mixture to the base of the pan with a spatula and leave to cook for 1 minute. Flip like an omelette and repeat.

Serve with some fresh parsley on top. For Nigel's packed lunch, I also made this mix into burger shaped patties which are delicious eaten cold with some of our homemade green tomato chutney.

Unstoppable Courgettes

The courgettes/marrow still showed no sign of slowing down in size or numbers. We were eating them in stir fries, as a side vegetable, making chutney, wine, and now we were preparing them for the freezer. Despite reading that it was not a successful idea we were running out of options and needed to give it a try.

Courgettes have a notoriously bad reputation for being frozen and many people report that they deteriorate into a soggy mess when defrosted. Therefore, I knew that the courgettes we were freezing would only be suitable for certain dishes, principally soups, stew thickeners and sauces. That said I tried many of the methods I read about in an attempt to extend these meal options. These included freezing sautéed slices of courgette and cutting them into ribbons and tray freezing, etc. The other way to successfully freeze them was to make the dish containing the courgettes and freeze as a ready meal. These turned out to be great time-savers for Nigel when I went away for a week in September to visit Jaime in the UK for her 17th birthday. He had a ready supply of meals with no preparation need, well apart from he needed to remember to get them out of the freezer to defrost ready to cook as we did not have a microwave!

Making and freezing the soup turned out to be an ideal method of using large amounts of courgettes. This quick and easy soup, with add lots of homegrown garlic added to ward off colds and flu with winter approaching, was a favourite of ours

Courgette and potato soup

Ingredients:

600g potatoes peeled and sliced

3 large cloves of garlic chopped

Seasoning

3 large courgettes

Basil and mint (you can use any combination of herbs)

Cayenne pepper

Method

Place the potatoes in saucepan and cover with 1.5 pints of water. Bring to the boil and skim off any foam that comes to the surface.

Add the chopped garlic and simmer for 10 minutes until the potatoes are soft. Remove from the heat and mash the potatoes and garlic in the cooking water.

Add the grated or chopped courgettes and return the soup to the heat. Simmer for 5 minutes until the courgettes are soft. Season to taste.

Serve with a dash of olive oil on the top and some roughly chopped basil and mint. This is a hearty soup which is a perfect autumn lunch served with some homemade bread.

Another great use for the courgette and any early pumpkins is a healthy vegetarian favourite of ours:

Vegetable curry

Ingredients:

Olive oil

1 onion peeled and chopped

2 gloves of garlic

1 large courgette sliced

500g pumpkin diced

100g mushrooms quartered

1 red or green pepper

150g broccoli or cauliflower

600 ml of curry sauce (homemade or jar)

400 ml water.

Method

Place the vegetable oil in a large saucepan and fry the onion slowly for 5 -10 minutes till soft not brown.

Add all other vegetables and stir through the oil and onion mix.

Add the curry sauce and simmer for 20 minutes do not overcook as the vegetables will develop a mashed potato appearance.

Add water as required to get the consistency you like as it can thicken quickly as the vegetables cook.

Serve with rice or a baguette. Garnish with coriander or Italian parsley.

As we continued to harvest and eat our vegetables, we were producing a large amount of garden waste in terms of the foliage. Some if it was suitable for the cockerel, chicken, ducks and rabbit, but most had to be cut up for the compost bin. The sweetcorn which until late July had looked like tall sunflowers with no flowers had grown numerous cobs laden with plump kernels and by mid-September they were ready for eating. Once the cobs were removed there was a lot of waste, but fortunately, the rabbit and the ducks enjoyed picking and pulling at the long stems and the sweetcorn tassels.

Sweet corn patties

Ingredients:

400g sweetcorn kernels

125g self-rising flour

2 eggs

2 onion or some leeks

1 tbsp chopped coriander

5 tbsp milk

4 tbs olive oil

Method

Mix all of the ingredients, excluding 1 tablespoon of olive or vegetable oil, in a bowl with a spatula then season. The mix should be firm enough for you to handle it to form the patties. If it's too wet, sieve some flour in and mix again.

Divide the mixture into 10-12 small balls and then gently flatten each one. Heat the remaining 1 tablespoon of olive or vegetable oil in a frying pan and place the patties in the pan. Cook each side for 3 minutes on medium heat each side until crisp, add more oil if needed to prevent burning and sticking.

These make a tasty lunch box snack or a tasty addition to salad meal. We also premade them for BBQ's when the children visited. They can be dipped in salsa or homemade relish.

Included at our children's insistence -My Parents and the Magic Mushrooms.

The title of this story said like that sounds like the title of a children's book, but the story is far removed from a children's tale. However, it still has our children, as old as they are, in fits of laughter. I did not want to include the story in this book, and I deliberately only alluded to it in 'Two dogs and a suitcase'. However, as my eldest daughter Samantha reminded me, "You can't just exclude stories that make you look or sound silly otherwise the readers don't see the real you." When did she become so wise and noble?

So here it is. Our first mushroom encounter came at the end of September 2012 shortly after arriving in France. We were walking the boys as we do every morning, and we noticed mushrooms growing on the grass bank beside the brook that runs alongside the village green. They had appeared overnight, and we were intrigued. Obviously we knew that not all mushrooms are edible and so we didn't pick any. When we walked the boys later that day all the mushrooms were gone. We thought, 'Oh maybe they were edible after all because someone has picked them.' The next morning another crop of mushrooms had appeared and this time not wanting to miss out we picked some. As we were unprepared for this foraging mission, we filled our coat pockets, and I held a few in my hands. As we returned home, we met Andre and the Deputy Maire and in my usual pigeon French I tried to ask about the mushrooms and whether they were safe to eat. The consensus was that if the underside was rouge (pink) and not blanc (white) then they were safe to eat. The mushrooms we had picked met that criteria so we took them home convinced that we had a nice addition to our meal for that evening which was roast vegetables as we were still vegetarian at that time.

That evening Nigel prepared the mushrooms and added them to the roasting dish. Everything looked normal but as the cooking commenced a strange odour came from the oven but because the oven was still relatively new we didn't suspect the mushrooms. When the meal was cooked, even though the mushrooms now resembled black slimy lumps, we ate them. Everyone has heard or read stories about people eating so called 'magic mushrooms' that result in strange mental side-effects. The fact that we started discussing this over dinner made me wonder if what happened next was psychosomatic. From the time we ate them strange, but nonspecific things started to happen especially when we went to bed.

Always the optimist I put my 'symptoms', as I now call them, down to eating a big meal with red wine too close to going bed. I felt overly full and bloated in my stomach, to the point of not knowing if I needed to be sick or if I needed to go and sit on the toilet! This preyed on my mind, and I had the sensation of wanting to go to sleep, but I was afraid of what might happen if I did. Although I felt as if I was awake, I am not sure whether it was dreaming or hallucinations, but I had images of this black sludge resembling the mushrooms oozing from my body. This horrific vision woke or disturbed me several times, and it was the worst night's sleep, if you can call it that, I had had in a long time. I was not sick, and no black sludge left my body but I felt too embarrassed to discuss it with Nigel who in the morning appeared to be fine.

On our morning walk, we collected more mushrooms, but as we cooked them that evening, the smell resurrected the previous night's dreaming sensations, and I knew I could not eat them again. I decided to share my experience with Nigel and guess what, he had had the same thing in his sleep but didn't want to say anything.

Some months later when I told my son Rob about it, he as a man of the world said, "Mum, that's hilarious it sounds like you'd been smoking weed." I felt a bit awkward discussing this, especially as all he was interested in is how long the effects lasted and did we enjoy it. He also could not contain his hysterical laughter, and when he visited soon after, he wanted to know if we could go mushroom picking. This is now a family joke as everyone knows about our mushroom encounter. When my daughter Samantha heard the story she just said, "Oh Mum, what are you like?" That did not stop her from laughing so much that she had to pull over as she was driving at the time! No, I didn't enjoy it and now they joke about mum and dad getting high on mushrooms in France to celebrate becoming empty nesters, like it's something we should be proud of.

The French take their wild mushroom foraging very seriously, and the government even has regulations and rules put in place for picking mushrooms. Fast forward to September 2013 and it is mushroom time again in France. Although we had been foraging throughout the summer, when then we spotted the mushrooms growing in the same spot as before I have to admit we were tempted. However, the memories and subsequent embarrassment of telling the children our story was enough to persuade us to let someone else enjoy a magic moment this year.

Not to be outdone by the mushrooms, we did achieve another self-sufficiency objective this summer, which was growing mushrooms using a kit that I bought from a French gardening magazine.

I thought this was very brave as I could barely understand the product description let alone the instructions. However, we managed it, and they thrived in their polystyrene boxes in our cave and we enjoyed many crops of white and brown mushrooms with no adverse effects!

Growing mushrooms that are safe to eat!

Chapter 9
October

As the last of the sunny days, reminiscent of summer, scattered themselves in the now autumnal weather we were aware of the urgency of completing the harvest of our remaining vegetables. The pumpkins had completely taken over the bottom of the garden. They had sent their tendrils across the brook into Yvette's meadow and despite our best efforts over the summer to retrain them back into our garden they had delicately embedded their fruits into the grassy bank. Their fruits, which when first formed from the golden flowers that preceded them resembled fragile Christmas tree decorations were now mutated and monstrous spherical objects with shells that looked and felt as if they could resist bullets. They were so heavy that only Nigel could lift them. The heaviest pumpkin during our harvest this year was 16kgs.

Pumpkin is an awesome vegetable. We ate the seeds as healthy snacks, used the shell for Halloween lanterns or fed them in chunks to the ducks.

The flesh we used as chips for a potato alternative; filling for pumpkin pie; chunks in a curry and grated for pumpkin chilli-con-carne. It is such a great all-rounder food and to think I didn't like it before we moved to France. My reluctance to even try it came as a result of being given some undercooked pumpkin in my youth. The memory of that hard, chewy substance that stuck to my teeth like an unripe banana was all that was needed to make sure I didn't try it again. However, after being resistant to ever trying it again ever, having a pumpkin curry with my new friend and neighbour Julia when we arrived in France made me realise that I love this food. All those years I had missed out, but no more.

George tries to help prepare the pumpkins for storing

We were in pumpkin heaven as we harvested 22 supersize pumpkins which had perfect thick skins enabling them to be stored with ease for use over the winter months. We discovered a very simple technique to prevent mould. Wipe them over with a weak bleach solution and allow to air dry. Ta dah! No mould. So let's eat:

Pumpkin curry

Ingredients:

Pumpkins diced into 1 inch cubes

½ pint stock

1 onion

3 cloves garlic grated

1 tbs curry powder

Olive oil

1 red chilli- finely chopped

Fresh coriander

Seasoning

Method

Heat the oil in a deep frying pan; add the curry powder to form a paste.

Add the finely chopped onion, grated garlic and chopped chilli with ¾ of the fresh coriander.

Blend in the pan with a wooden spoon for 1 minute.

Add the pumpkin cubes and season.

Coat the pumpkin in the paste before adding the stock and simmering for 15 - 20 minutes.

Serve with rice and garnish with fresh coriander

Pumpkin dumplings (my guilty pleasure)

Ingredients:

200g grated pumpkin

50g flour

50 g margarine

1 tsp baking powder

Thyme

Seasoning

1 egg

Dash of milk

Method

Place the grated pumpkin and baking powder in a large bowl and mix.

Add the flour a little at a time until soft dough starts to form.

Using a wet spoon take a spoonful of the dough and gently place it in a saucepan of boiling salted water.

Continue until all of the dumplings are in the water. Depending on the size of the dumplings, allow them to boil for about 10 minutes. You can test them by putting a sharp knife into the centre. If the knife comes out clean then, they are cooked. Drain in a colander and separate immediately.

It depends on the meal with which you are having with the dumplings, but you could replace the boiling element of this recipe by placing the dumplings directly into the casserole or stew. With this method, the dumplings will absorb moisture from the casserole causing them to spread out to form a layer on the top.

Alternatively you can have them as side-dish.- se the boiling method, and then place them in a shallow frying pan with some olive oil. Sauté for 5 minutes or just long enough to colour them. We served ours with some grated cheese or herbs on top. They are also delicious cold; we sliced them and ate them with green tomato chutney and cheese as a lunchtime bread alternative. Another great use for them is as emergency croutons for soup.

I think you can probably understand how I became addicted to them. I always made sure that I had at least six in the freezer for emergencies, on standby as they made a good accompaniment to many other foods and dishes.

It's not all fruit and vegetables there are nuts too!

October is also chestnut time. As we arrived in France in late September 2012, we witnessed chestnut time soon after arriving, however we were unprepared to indulge in it, unlike our French neighbours. Yvette and her family went out in convoy and returned with sacks full of chestnuts. It was a big family affair as they grouped together to release them from their prickly cases and prepare them for cooking, etc. It must be a Mediterranean trait as the whole extended family sat outdoors chatting, laughing and preparing food or ingredients while the grandchildren ran around laughing and playing. It was a scene reminiscent of an Italian pizza sauce advertisement on television. I must admit that before we witnessed the family involved in this activity we saw that she had a pile of chestnuts at the side of the house. Yvette drove off every morning and every evening and was gone for 30 minutes each time. We thought maybe she had a horse or an animal of some description and that she was collecting the chestnuts for animal feed. We later discovered that her twice daily visits were to her husband's grave in the Chirac cemetery. Yvette was an experienced cook who owned and ran the local café, which was now her home, for many years. Therefore, it was no surprise when delicious nutty aromas started wafting from her kitchen proving that these chestnuts were for eating.

At that time I had no idea how many recipes there were for using chestnuts, both sweet and savoury. Our modest effort at collecting them on that first attempt meant that we did manage to gather enough for roasting on the top of the wood burner in our crepe pan. However, in October 2013 with a more in-depth knowledge of our local area, we knew that we were surrounded by many chestnuts trees. These were located in the back lanes where we walked the boys and a track by the local 'stade' (playing field.) We were confident of having a plentiful supply of this nutritious and tasty ingredient. I had done my research and had recipes planned for now and over Christmas. Obviously I would need to practice the recipes for taste and experimentation purposes, but that is one of the perks of being cook!

Collecting the chestnuts was a prickly task, but pretty easy. We would take a bucket each and our gardening gloves, which as it happened, were no good against the harsh spikes protecting the delicious nut kernels. We were surprised how many we managed to collect. However, it quickly became apparent when we sat down each evening to peel and prepare these nuts, how long it took. We were also careful to watch for maggots as they were apt at burrowing in undetected as we sometimes ended up peeling and preparing in the twilight. Here are some of the recipes which we tried and enjoyed.

Chestnut loaf

Ingredients:

2 tsp butter/margarine or oil

1 large onion

2 celery sticks (we didn't have celery, so I omitted them)

2 lbs of peeled and cooked chestnuts

2 tbs chopped fresh parsley

2 tbs lemon juice (optional)

1 clove garlic

For the crispy topping

Fresh breadcrumbs

¼ cup of olive oil

Method

Boil the peeled chestnuts for 7 minutes.

Melt the butter/margarine (if using) or add the oil to a frying pan.

Sauté the onion until soft not brown on a low heat.

Transfer to a large mixing bowl.

Drain the previously cooked chestnuts.

Mash or coarsely blend then adding the parsley and garlic.

Brush a loaf tin with oil and then press the mixture into the tin with the back of a spoon

If applying the crispy topping add a layer of bread crumbs and drizzle of oil and season before cooking for 30 minutes on medium heat.

You may need to add some extra oil during cooking as the chestnuts absorb all moisture

An alternative topping that we tried was to grate potato in a bowl, mix with some melted butter until coated, place this on the loaf mix, season and drizzle with oil then bake. This gives a rosti style topping and some extra crunch. We ate this as a main meal with vegetables and also sliced cold with salad

Chestnut and red wine paté

We researched and adapted this recipe ready to make it as a Christmas meal starter, although we had to make some to sample beforehand for quality control purposes you understand.

Ingredients:

100g chopped chestnuts (cooked weight)

100g chestnut purée

1 tbsp olive oil

1 small onion, chopped

1 clove of garlic, crushed

Dried thyme

75g homemade breadcrumbs

1 tbsp alcohol, we used homebrew white wine, but you can choose any you have available.

150ml red wine (Cheap wine is fine)

150ml vegetable stock

Seasoning

Method

In a large saucepan pour in the olive oil and cook the chopped onion and garlic with the thyme until soft not brown.

Pour in slowly the stock and red wine in slowly, stirring continuously until it comes to the boil.

Remove from the heat and spoon in the chopped chestnuts, chestnut purée, bread crumbs, and the additional alcohol.

Season and return to the heat and cook slowly until it thickens to a paste consistency.

To serve, we used white ramekins to show off the colouring of the slightly red paté at Christmas with a sprig of coriander to garnish. When we served it to the children as they visited on various dates over Christmas they thought we had bought it and said it looked 'really special.'

At Christmas, we ate our pate with crackers and side salad as a light supper after a huge Christmas lunch, on four occasions due to the children all visiting at different times. It keeps nicely in the fridge, and

I think it tasted better for being prepared in advance and chilled.

Growing peanuts update:

Our peanut tree had grown, in size, to a little under a foot in height. It had lost the delicate yellow flowers of the summer, and it appeared barren and still no nuts had grown. One evening after a flash flood while we were out walking the boys, we came home to mop up indoors and make fork holes in the ground to disperse the flooded ground and discovered that peanuts grow underground! There they were now exposed as the soil had been washed away. The peanuts were underground all the time, who knew? We certainly didn't, I always assumed monkey nuts or peanuts hung on trees. We dug some up and there they were, proper peanuts. We had grown peanuts in France, how awesome is that?

Home-brew by Nigel October update:

18th October was a momentous day in the homebrew calendar. It saw the bottling of the homemade wine, which had been fermenting or bubbling or just doing something in my kitchen for the last few weeks. As Nigel bottled it there was half a bottle spare, so we put it into the fridge. That evening we couldn't resist having a taste, even though we knew we were supposed to leave it to settle and to improve. It was awesome; if it tasted this good now it would be an excellent vintage by Christmas!!

Chapter 10
Preparing for Christmas

As the summer and autumn of 2013 drew to a close, we were stocked up for winter. We had home grown produce in the cold store, including onions, garlic, potatoes and pumpkins. The freezer was full of new potatoes, courgette dishes, courgette cake, haricot verte, peas, sweetcorn and pumpkin puree. In boxes in the bedroom we had multiple jars of jams, preserves and pickles made from green tomatoes, cucumbers, blackberries, rhubarb, plums and radishes. It was a great feeling to have so much food available after having been through such frugal times, although there was never a feeling of being extravagant or greedy as everything that was stored had taken a lot of hard work to achieve. However, the greatest feeling was that of satisfaction, knowing that we had grown it in our secret garden in South West rural France. We knew that Christmas would be an extended affair this year, and we would be having a family Christmas spread over four occasions throughout December and into January.

We decided in October that our meat for Christmas would be two of the male ducks, allowing half a duck for each of the Christmas meals. After trying to buy two males and two females for breeding, we had ended up with three males and one female despite extensive research and advice from an English speaking breeder. This combination led to unrest in the duck enclosure and so choosing two males for slaughter was not difficult. We picked the two with the most attitude and aggression, our aim being to keep the one female and the best-behaved male to be her mate.

Undeterred by the size of these birds and despite my arthritis weakened wrists we devised a plan for preparing these birds for the table. I consulted my copy of 'Storey's Guide to Raising Ducks' and we set up the utility area in the barn to be able to accommodate these birds which were three times bigger than the cockerels. Although Nigel had one experience of killing an annoying chicken, this part of our lifestyle choice was usually my task. However, on this occasion he reluctantly agreed to help.

Four ducks and a chicken!

In early December with the first duck caught and in the barn the process became a noisy and difficult affair as I obviously did not have enough strength in my wrists. We did not want the birds to suffer in this process and realised that the next one had to be done differently.

With the first one done, the second one caught us by surprise when one wing escaped our grip and hit me in the left breast. Despite the pain, I tried to regain some control while Nigel rugby tackled the duck to prevent it escaping into the garden where the boys were ready and waiting to pounce. As the feathers and sawdust from our wood chopping area settled we looked at each other and both said, "Never again." We stood there and looked at each other, Nigel holding the duck and me holding my left breast. Returning the duck to the enclosure, we went indoors only to be attacked by George, our kitten who was attracted to smell of a duck. Later that afternoon the local feral cats broke into the barn to attack the sack that was covering the hanging bird. Luckily 'our boys' alerted us to the intruders, and we were able to save the duck from being dragged away.

Nigel and Clair enjoying a Christmas meal of Roast duck and home grown vegetables

For our Christmas meal, we served dishes made from our homegrown and foraged foods. Our starter was chestnut and red wine paté with savoury crackers garnished with home grown herbs. The main course was roast duck, roast potatoes cooked in duck fat, boiled new potatoes and a selection of vegetables from our garden. This was served with bread sauce made from home-made bread crumbs, and chestnut stuffing balls and gravy. For pudding, we had pumpkin pie and courgette cake with custard.

Sarah Jane's Bread sauce

Ingredients:

½ pint of milk

1 small onion, peeled and halved

2 cloves

50g of breadcrumbs

Seasoning

Method:

Put the milk, onion halves and cloves in a saucepan. Place on a low heat and bring to a simmer.

After 30 minutes remove the onion halves and cloves and add the bread crumbs, continue to simmer until it reaches a sauce consistency.

Season to taste.

Remove from the heat and serve in a warm dish

As we continue with our French experience, the plans for our garden and our lifestyle are evolving. Everything that we have experienced will shape the decisions and plans for the future. The moral of our story is that living on a frugal budget does not mean sacrificing on taste or variety.

We hope you have enjoyed sharing 'Our Frugal Summer in Charente' and that you will enjoy some of the recipes that we have included.

About the author

Author Sarah Jane Butfield was born in Ipswich and raised in rural Suffolk, UK. Sarah Jane is a wife, mother, ex-qualified nurse and now an internationally published author. Married three times with four children, three stepchildren and two playful Australian Cattle dogs she an experienced modern day mum to her 'Brady bunch', but she loves every minute of their convoluted lives.

Sarah Jane the roving Florence Nightingale fulfilled her childhood dream of becoming a nurse and went on to use her nursing and later teaching qualifications to take her around the world. She is now an International Best Selling author of two travel memoirs set in Australia and France, with this and another non-fiction book scheduled for release in November 2014.

Glass Half Full: Our Australian Adventure, her debut travel memoir, and the sequel Two dogs and a suitcase: Clueless in Charente, are regularly found high in the Amazon rankings. Categories include Parenting, Grief, Christian faith, Step-parenting, Travel and France.

Thank you for reading.

Books by Sarah Jane Butfield

Glass Half Full: Our Australian Adventure

Is the glass half-empty or half full? Ironically, sometimes life influences our view and alters our perception. Life changing events, up to 1997, almost destroyed me. At my lowest point, and just in time, I met Nigel. He helped me to discover how a positive attitude can change everything. I decided not to squander any more of my time or energy on undeserving people. This new positive approach helps me to perceive my glass as half-full, with my aim being to achieve a happy and healthy life for my family. Together, we live life to the full. In 2008, with good times ahead of us, my glass was half-full. As a family, we made the biggest and most difficult decision of our lives; part of our family would immigrate to Australia. We lived the Australian dream; embracing the adventure until adversity came to test us. A sequence of life changing events including, a close family bereavement, PTSD (Post Traumatic Stress Disorder) following a road rage car accident and the shock of losing the roots to our Australian adventure as a result of the Brisbane floods tested us on many levels. Glass Half Full follows our journey into happy, sad and challenging times. Find out what it takes to survive with the odds stacked against you. Do you fight back, and if so, at what cost physically and emotionally? Could we maintain our positivity and family values against the odds? This is our story. books2read.com/GlassHalfFull

Two Dogs And A Suitcase: Clueless In Charente

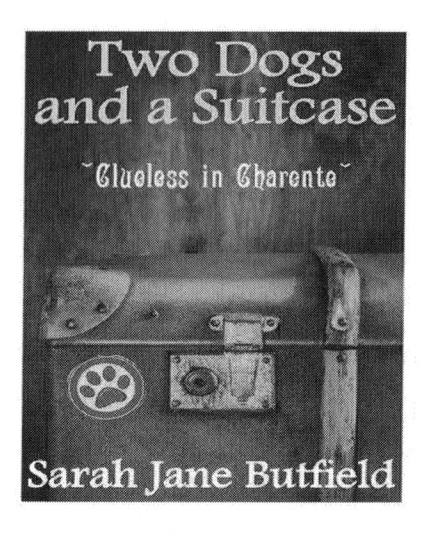

The title says it all: what we have and where we are. This book, the sequel to Glass Half Full: Our Australian Adventure, follows our French exploits as we endeavour to rebuild our lives in another new country, after spending four and half years in Australia. Our goal, or hope for the immediate future, is to focus positively on the present, so that we can start a new, optimistic future back in Europe. Our main aim is to be nearer to the children, leaving the dark clouds of the challenges we faced in Australia as a distant memory. Journey with us as we arrive in rural South West France; enjoy my reflections, thoughts, and observations about my family, our new surroundings, and our lifestyle. Follow the journey of my writing career and how we start our renovation project while managing our convoluted family life. Once again, we will laugh, cry, and enjoy life to the fullest with a generous helping of positive spin thrown in for good measure.

Read our story....books2read.com/TwoDogs

****

Other Books By Sarah Jane Butfield
What, Why, Where, When, Who & How Book Promotion Series
All links available on www.sarahjanebutfield.com

The Accidental Author
Permanently FREE

This is book 1 in a new series which looks at self-publishing for beginners and the skills needed for ongoing book marketing and promotion. This e-books series is based on the experiences of author Sarah Jane Butfield who writes travel memoirs, non-fiction books and romance short stories.

The Accidental Author introduces the author and this series of self-help e-books for new or aspiring self-published authors. The introduction starts with how and why Sarah Jane came to write and self-publish Glass Half Full: Our Australian Adventure. Find out how an aspiring author aims to be discovered while learning on the job how to write, publish and launch a new career in writing.

"Sarah Jane's never give up approach to life and anything she turns her hand to is beyond admirable." John Roberts

"A must read for any aspiring author or readers interested in the life of a self-published author. Sarah Jane's never give up approach to life and anything she turns her hand to is beyond admirable."

Book 2 The Amateur Authorpreneur

The Amateur Authorpreneur is a beginners' guide for authors who intend to develop their writing into a business, addressing the important task of book promotion and marketing. We look at laying the foundations of the authorpreneur book promotion toolkit, building a fan base on social media and much more.

You've written a book or you plan to - what do you need to consider?

What does it offer readers?

Why will they buy it?

Where are your readers?

When will you publish it?

Who are you?

How do you promote it!

Find out how to take the business of being an author up a gear to become an authorpreneur. The Amateur Authorpreneur will describe, using the What, Why Where, When, Who & How template, the process of taking the first steps into combining the craft of being an author with the business of marketing your work. Here are some beta reader comments:

"Aspiring authors will feel reassured that whatever their age or IT ability all of the skills needed to become an authorpreneur are achievable."

A non-author beta reader said, "I have discovered skills and tips that now helps me in both my personal and professional social media interactions."

"An avid reader who enjoys the work of indie authors was, "amazed at what's involved behind the scenes."

Book 3 The Intermediate Authorpreneur

"This guide is just what I needed to set my goals for the future"

"I am awe of what an indie author has to know and do on a daily basis, as a reader I applaud you all."

"A valuable guide and essential reading for all new authors or those that need to refocus their social media presence"

"The evidence based graphs and statistics were a nice, reassuring touch. Sarah definitely keeps it real."

Find out how to get your writing business started in easy to follow, simple steps which breaks down the fears and myths of social media and networking for aspiring and new authors. It's not rocket science and anyone can do it! Get started today and feel free to network with the author for additional support on your book marketing and promotional journey.

The Nomadic Nurse Series

Book One

'Ooh Matron!' is the first book in The Nomadic Nurse Series. Each book in the series takes you on a journey through medical specialisms and environments that formed part of Sarah Jane's nursing career. Throughout the series Sarah Jane uses her trademark honest and entertaining writing style to share insights into her thoughts, reflections and the changes in her personal life and circumstances as she moves forward in her career.

*****Award Winning Nurse Memoir*****

I am not sure what Florence Nightingale would have made of Sarah Jane! The story starts with a sixteen-year-old country girl who, for no apparent reason at the time, suddenly decided that she wanted to be a nurse. Sarah Jane was entering adulthood with no obvious career path in sight. She had planned a traditional, some would say old fashioned, future. Her vision was to leave school, find a job in a local store, get married and eventually have children.

Then everything changed, as she embarked on a journey which would help to map out her future by offering opportunities in a variety of places and healthcare settings. Find out how Sarah Jane deals with births, deaths and everything in between with laughter, tears and humility in this touching, sometimes heartrending, superbly written memoir.

5-star reviewers say:

"I laughed out loud at the hilarious antics, and was sobered by the genuine emotional moments that all health professionals will recognise. This is a book that will make you laugh and cry and you'll feel better for it - The perfect prescription."

"This funny, yet poignant nursing memoir has Sarah Jane's trademark honest writing style which shines through in every story she tells. From starting her student nurse training in Essex to coping with patients in happy, sad and heart-breaking situations. It gives you a young woman's view into the realities of entering the world of nursing in the 1980's. A highly entertaining and informative memoir which was able to take me from laughing out loud to having welled tears of empathy."

At all good bookstores on this link books2read.com/OohMatron

Book Two: Bedpans To Boardrooms

Due for release in December 2016

To hear about my latest books first, sign up for my exclusive mailing list.

http://eepurl.com/0IuML

Made in the USA
Charleston, SC
11 November 2016